ADVANCE PRAISE FOR CREATING EXCELLENCE

"For any leader or aspiring leader, this book offers a blueprint for navigating hostile territory and accelerating your journey." - *Admiral Mike Manazir (Retired) Top Gun Fighter Pilot, Commander of the USS Nimitz, and best-selling author*

"Bentley Nettles takes the experiences from a lifetime of service to his country and community and distills core takeaways for success. His formula for excellence is rooted in practical examples from his true-life experience." - *Karen Bonnarigo, Co-Founder and Winemaker, Messina Hof Winery, messinahof.com*

"As he shares his unique perspective, Bentley Nettles emphasizes the universal importance of selfless service and a commitment to a greater good." - *Col (R) Russ (Doc) Kotwal, 75th Ranger Battalion surgeon and Ranger Hall of Fame inductee*

"A great read by a great American. You don't have to be in the military or law enforcement to benefit from Bentley Nettles' practical leadership lessons." - *Andrew Nelson, Co-Founder and CEO of Lisam America, Board Member, Philanthropist and Civic Leader*

"A powerful look at leadership, from someone who's walked the walk. General Nettles shares new insights designed to help current and aspiring leaders to discover a pathway to growth." - *Kent Hance, Esq., Former Texas State Senator, US Congressman, Chancellor of the Texas Tech University System and Chairman of the Texas Railroad Commission*

"Being a leader can sometimes feel like you are in enemy territory. *Creating Excellence* shows you how to turn enemies into friends, navigating with insight from someone who's been there." - *Emily Knight, Ph.D. - Director of the Texas Restaurant Association*

"Bentley Nettles understands that legacies are not given, they are built. Can there be a higher aspiration for any leader?" - *Michael E. Caudle, Ph.D. Lieutenant Colonel, USA (Ret)*

"What's missing in the pursuit of excellence isn't the how to, it's the want to. Enable inspiration, and you've tapped into creating excellence. Read Bentley Nettles' book and be inspired." - *Christopher Bellavita, Ph.D. Director of Programs for the Naval Postgraduate School's Center for Homeland Defense and Security*

CREATING EXCELLENCE

INSIGHTS INTO LEADERSHIP, LIFE AND LEGACY

BENTLEY NETTLES, BRIGADIER GENERAL (BVT)

CONTENTS

PUBLISHED BY: BOOP HILL ENTERPRISES

PO BOX 313

WELLBORN, TX 77881

ISBN: 978-8-218-50922-4

FIRST EDITION: OCTOBER 2024

CHAPTER IMAGES BY MACROVECTOR ON FREEPIK, USED WITH PERMISSION.

To Tracy, Peter and Henry

It all begins with you

CREATING EXCELLENCE

"A true leader has the confidence to stand alone, the courage to make tough decisions, and the compassion to listen to the needs of others. He does not set out to be a leader but becomes one by the equality of his actions and integrity of his intent."

– General Douglas MacArthur

PROLOGUE

Where do you find excellence?

When we see something work, if it's working well, we see excellence. But excellence is also an attitude - an approach to life, and work, and relationships, that defines your character. And creates excellence for those around you.

Because the way you do one thing is the way you do everything.

That "one thing" means who you are. Who you are defines what you do. That's why we are called "human beings" not "human doings". But, as leaders, it often feels like we get lost inside of what we are doing - instead of seeking excellence inside ourselves. Creating excellence begins with character, as a starting point. Leadership starts with who you are. How you show up. And how deeply you can serve your team.

CAPTAIN CHARLIE PLUMB was shot down on his 75th mission. He ejected from his F-4 Phantom Jet while traveling at 600 knots (just under the speed of sound), rocketing through the skies near Hanoi. He parachuted to safety, captured by the Vietcong upon landing. He found himself imprisoned for 2,103 days in a North Vietnamese prisoner of war camp. He lived in an eight-by-eight cell, under unimaginable circumstances, until his release.

One night, after his return to the States, he was out at a restaurant having dinner. From two tables away, a man kept looking at him. "You're Charlie Plumb," said the stranger, pointing a finger at him.

"Yessir," Plumb said. "Yes, I am."

Standing to approach the captain's table, the man said, "You came out of that Top Gun outfit in Miramar, California." Plumb was taken aback. In the days after the Vietnam war ended, there was no internet. Plumb's background was not public information. So, how did this guy know his story?

"You were stationed on the aircraft carrier Kitty Hawk," he continued, batting 1.000. "You parachuted into enemy hands and were imprisoned in Vietnam for six years," the man said. Getting even more specific, he almost shouted, "You flew F-4 Phantom jets!"

"That's right," Plumb said, astonished. "But who are you?"

"I packed your parachute," the man said.

Excellence can be found inside of teams. Inside of organizations. Inside of you.

Even inside a parachute.

"I'm alive today," Plumb said, as he shook the man's hand in gratitude, "because of you."

As tough as it was in that prison, Plumb never would have survived if it wasn't for the work of this one individual - someone who, until now, the captain had never even met. Someone who cared about creating excellence.

WHO'S PACKING YOUR PARACHUTE?

And whose parachute is in your hands, right now?

Excellence is something that we all need. And that we all want.

Because everybody loves a winner.

We love to be associated with a winning team. There's nothing better than playing on a winning team - whether your goal has a net around it, or an annual report tied to it. Helping others to succeed - helping the team to win - is the key to our own personal success. Inside the mission, we create excellence.

That excellence comes from dedication, from commitment, and from discipline. The good news is: we all possess those characteristics, and those capabilities. We all know excellence when we see it, when we feel it, and when we see the outcomes that we want.

There are three simple ways to create excellence. These principles will guide every chapter in this book, and - if you are truly creating excellence - they will guide you, on your journey.

Your journey of impact.

Your journey of service.

Your journey of leadership.

I could take some space here in this prologue to tell you about myself, maybe offer up an anecdote about my brother, or tell you how much I love my wife. But instead, let me focus on what really matters. Let me share with you why I wrote this book.

I went back to my team - a team from a well-known agency, in my home state, The Texas Alcoholic Beverage Commission (TABC) - and I asked them, "What were three things we accomplished, while I was here?" I wanted to recognize them, not me. I wanted to recognize excellence.

What they told me formed the foundation of this book. As I reflected on the ideas from my team, I knew that I had to share them. I knew that the best recognition of excellence is passing it along to others.

A time of transition is a time of reflection. Here are my reflections, as I moved on from my commission - reprinted here exactly as I shared it, upon my transition:

"All good things must come to an end" are the words attributed to General George S. Patton in 1945 during his final change of command ceremony. He rightly went on to acknowledge his soldiers, "The best thing that has ever happened to me thus far is the honor and privilege of having commanded the Third Army." I too am so fortunate to have similar sentiments during service and about you on this occasion.

The best thing that has happened to me to date, by far, has been the honor and privilege of serving our state as the 14th Executive Director of the Texas Alcoholic Beverage Commission, and most especially to have served with all of you.

Thank you so much for your hard work, your innovation and your professionalism. From where we were as an agency in the summer of 2017 to today, this has been an incredible success story. You have made a difference. We have accomplished many great things during my tenure as your Executive Director, such as:

- **TABC LEADS Initiative** — The first TABC leadership development course developed and implemented by our own employees.
- **Criminal Intelligence Unit** — Created with your help and know-how to support investigations into organized crime, drug trafficking and human trafficking.
- **The Target Responsibility for Alcohol-Connected Emergencies (TRACE) Unit** — You helped create and successfully implement a statewide TRACE unit,

which has so far achieved an average administrative and criminal prosecution rate of 25% of traffic-related fatalities or serious injury resulting from businesses overserving or selling alcohol to minors.

- **Constituent Relations Course** — You helped implement best practices for customer relations fundamentals adapted from the Disney models to improve the TABC customer experience.
- **Texas Responsible Alcohol Delivery (TRAD) Course** — This initiative trains delivery drivers to know their responsibility when delivering alcohol to residences.
- **Public-Private Partnership with Beer Distributors** — Your innovative approach enhanced awareness of human trafficking statewide and directly led to a 70% increase in human trafficking complaints into the agency. Since September 2019, TABC has investigated 494 allegations of human trafficking, and discovered 103 violations — resulting in 31 administrative violations and 72 criminal charges filed.
- **Victim Services Coordinator** — Your vision resulted in the creation of this position to facilitate service coordination to victims of human trafficking as quickly as possible. Your accomplishment assists victims in breaking free of their trafficker. Since bringing the victim services coordinator on board, 76 potential victims have been referred to the VSC, 24 of whom disclosed being victims of sex trafficking.
- **TABC Hall of Honor** — You helped develop and implement the TABC Hall of Honor to publicly acknowledge the legacy left by former employees whose vision and hard work were game changers for the agency's path and trajectory.

- **TABC Honor Guard** — Together, we created and deployed the TABC Honor Guard to extend honor and dignity to those former employees of the agency who choose to be so recognized. The Honor Guard also reinforces the professionalism of our Law Enforcement Division.

- **Hurricane Harvey Response** — Peace officers and staff from TABC teamed up with our brothers and sisters in law enforcement statewide during Hurricane Harvey. It was the first complete deployment of our law enforcement division in support of Texas emergency management efforts. You made a difference at an especially meaningful moment.

- **Personnel Early Notification System** — TABC's Law Enforcement Division adopted the use of the Guardian Software System to better identify potential harmful patterns by employees. The division could then intervene at the earliest possible moment to correct the behavior, assist the employee, and identify positive behavior to assist in development of the employee as a potential future leader in the organization.

- **Empowering Texas Veterans Program** — You saw the need to assist veteran entrepreneurs in the alcoholic beverage industry and worked collaboratively with other state agencies to foster mentor relationships with established business owners.

- **Ports of Entry Training Standardization** — You developed a field training officer program for regulatory compliance officers to ensure standardized training is provided to all POE employees, the impact of which was seen in increased tax collection and illegal alcohol seizures.

- **Reorganization of Licensing Division by Functional Requirements** — You saw the need to reorganize licensing along functional requirements of the licensing process, which resulted in a 38% increase in efficiency in workflow and product.
- **Grant Funding Success** — Beyond the TxDOT grant [Texas Department of Transportation] the agency typically qualifies for, through your hard work in FY 2021, TABC was awarded two new grants to strengthen human trafficking investigations and connect human trafficking victims to services.
- **Advanced Undercover School** — Through your hard work and vision of what TABC could become, you developed the curriculum for our Advanced Undercover School. The school is extremely complex and unique in many ways, not the least of which is its victim-centric approach. This has resulted in a higher degree of confidence and professionalism in our enforcement efforts to eradicate human trafficking from licensed locations.
- **Online TCOLE Human Trafficking Course** — You joined forces with the Texas A&M Engineering Extension Service (TEEX) and Texas Commission on Law Enforcement (TCOLE) to produce the new continuing education course that benefits law enforcement officers across the state. The course keeps Texas officers at the forefront of combating human trafficking by learning to recognize and investigate signs of human trafficking. By August of 2021, the course had nearly 13,000 enrollees.

- **Administrative Violations Warning-Based System** — Because of your innovative and collaborative approach to regulating industry, you developed a business-friendly, warning-based system for non-public safety related administrative violations to encourage business compliance.
- **Outstanding Agency Award from TxDOT and MADD** — TABC law enforcement's hard work to curtail underage drinking earned TABC the Outstanding Agency Award from TxDOT and the Southeast Texas chapter of MADD.
- **Online Commission Meetings** — Before the pandemic, your innovative work with industry allowed the agency to bring commission meetings and documents online so that more industry members and interested stakeholders could participate.
- **2young2drink Website** — Your vision for combating underage drinking online was reflected in the incredible work on the 2young2drink website, which resulted in a remarkable increase in visitors to the site. It was recognized with a coveted Gold Award from the American Association of Marketing and Communication Professionals (AMCP).
- **Improved Agency Communication and Engagement** — You held statewide industry roundtables, began new email campaigns, increased email open rates, and kept open lines of communication with industry and staff throughout the pandemic, historic legislative implementation, and technology transformation. Communications materials informed businesses, staff and the public. This includes an informational video on TABC's

mission to combat human trafficking that was also recognized as a finalist in the international Adobe Government Creativity Awards and won an Award of Distinction from the Communicator Awards.

- **TABC Public Website** — Your hard work on improving the agency's customer experience is reflected in the new website, which replaced a 20-year-old website. The redesigned tabc.texas.gov was recognized with a Gold Award in the 15th Annual AVA Digital Awards, an international competition sponsored and judged by AMCP. The website was also recognized by the Center for Plain Language with an Award of Distinction.

- **Operating in the Cloud** — The Innovation and Technology Division transitioned the agency from working at 5% in the cloud to greater than 80% in the cloud, meeting the Legislature's intent and creating a more mobile and agile workforce during the February freeze and pandemic. This allowed the agency to continue to operate and serve Texans.

- **Alcohol Industry Management System (AIMS) Development and Deployment** — Your hard work has allowed us to transition from 11 legacy systems to a new online way for customers to do business with the agency. Change is always stressful and frustrating for all involved. Your focus on customer service allowed you to continue to meet challenges and create ways for our customers to get online, submit their new permits and renew their current permits. Although not easy, I'm extremely proud of your hard work.

- **CAPPS HR Deployment and Implementation** — Your work to deploy CAPPS across the agency allowed employees greater access and flexibility in interfacing with TABC Human Resources.

- **Protecting Employees During the Pandemic** — You purchased, acquired and managed over 26,000 personal protective equipment items to ensure safety of agency personnel during COVID-19.

- **Rules** — You developed and maintained a multi-year plan to adopt rules to implement new laws and review existing rules. Out of 200 active rules at the inception of Strategic Initiatives and Performance Improvement (SIPI), more than 150 rules have been published by the commission. Efforts include reorganizing and streamlining rules for ease of understanding and transparency for industry. Established procedures included internal and external stakeholders in every step of the rule-making process.

- **Policies and Procedures** — You developed a standard approval process, templates, and numbering and abbreviations for internal policies, procedures, and forms. By creating and maintaining a plan to centralize and systematically review all TABC policies and procedures, more than 200 policies or procedures have been published in software and existing policies will be reviewed and updated to conform to new standards. You established procedure to outline involvement of multiple parties in the management, review, drafting, and approval phases and the technology involved for updates and distribution of policy and procedure documents.

- **Development of Standard Penalty Guidelines for Regulatory Violations** — Required by Sunset

legislation, new policy and rule were developed to
use a list of base penalties and employ a worksheet to
calculate penalties for regulatory violations,
including new authority to consider a permittee's
profits. The new methodology is more transparent to
industry and encourages consistent application
across all regions of the state.

These remarkable achievements were done during some of the most challenging times for the agency. I couldn't be prouder of these achievements and the agency's transformation.

Tracy and I are looking forward to whatever the next chapter God has planned for us. After 37 years of public service, both federal and state, it is time to let someone else take the ball and run with it. I look forward to reading about your continued accomplishments at TABC, and I will dearly miss my colleagues and friends in the TABC family, all of whom are deeply cherished.

GOD BLESS you and God bless Texas!

A. Bentley Nettles
Brigadier General (BVT) Retired,
14th Executive Director of the Texas Alcoholic Beverage Commission

1

THREE KEYS TO LEADERSHIP

There are three keys to leadership.

WAIT A MINUTE. Only three? Can it really be that simple, in creating excellence?

The answer to that question lies not only in the three keys, but in your willingness to commit, to invest in yourself, and to serve at a higher level.

Inside that commitment, excellence can be found, created, and shared.

Step one is sharing your vision.

That doesn't mean that you enter a room talking and telling people what to do. Giving orders is not sharing a vision. Even if the people in the room are there to carry out your orders.

Sharing your vision starts with something that's worth sharing. That means your vision begins with understanding. As you move through this book, look for new understanding.

As you move through your career, look to those around you

for new understanding. Find a coach, listen to mentors, accept advice from those you trust - because understanding is the key to your leadership vision.

And that vision is created with, through and for others. In the pages that follow, I'll show you in no uncertain terms how to find the resources you need, create the systems you want, and establish the vision that creates alignment. Because sharing your vision is about engagement. Getting others engaged, and enrolled, is fundamental to trust. And without trust, even the most well-thought-out vision isn't going to matter much. Because, behind every plan, is a person. Creating trust starts with your character, and we will explore how to turn integrity into a competitive advantage.

Step two is setting a standard - enabling people to do what needs to be done.

Step two is about empowerment, conversations, and standards. Set a standard and help people to reach that standard. As a leader, one of my proudest accomplishments was the development of a leadership training program for my team. Because creating excellence requires an environment where excellence is explored, described, demonstrated and delivered. How are you creating that standard, right now, to empower your team? And are you empowering yourself, right now, to do what needs to be done?

What are your standards? And how are you sharing that standard with the team? Expectations alone are not enough. Expectations require empowerment, and ownership - a shared ownership that is woven throughout the pages of this book. Train people to this standard.

Oftentimes what stops us isn't a knowledge gap, or a skills gap. We know what needs to be done. We know how to do it. And if we don't, there are coaches, manuals, web pages, training classes and YouTube videos to help.

What's missing isn't the how to.

It's the want to. Enable inspiration, and you've tapped into creating excellence.

Leadership isn't always easy. But it's often more straightforward, and simpler, than we realize. As the saying goes, "It's never tougher than it is in your mind." As you consider your leadership journey, look in the direction of two powerful words. Two words that can help you to do what needs to be done, to empower yourself to make the hard decisions, and to support your team on a deeper level. Here they are:

PERMISSION GRANTED.

Holding people accountable is the third step.

Which people, you may wonder? That's easy: start with yourself. You've made a commitment to this book. Make a commitment to yourself, to create excellence in every aspect of your life. This book will show you how. Set a standard, and hold people accountable to that standard. Accountability is key.

Discipline, whether it's reading a book or leading a Fortune 500 company, is simple. Discipline is remembering what you want. And wanting that thing more than the sting of regret, defeat and disappointment.

Choose excellence. As you read each chapter, begin with an intention. An intention to discover something new. Make excellence your standard, teach others how to achieve it, and hold them accountable.

Inside the stories that I share, you will see yourself. You will see that these are not tales of a superhero (far from it!) but the tales of someone just like you. Maybe my circumstances were different, my experiences unique, but the principles of leadership remain unfazed by outside scenarios.

I am someone who was called to lead. Someone who wanted to serve. That service took me to careers in the military, to working as a lawyer, and serving as the leader of a large state agency. As far as my next chapter is concerned, well, for that you'll have to turn the page.

But for now: commit to yourself. And recognize that excellence is closer than you might think. Because *Creating Excellence* is in your hands. Are you ready for the journey to begin?

2

THE 90 DAY PLAN

"It's what you learn after you know it all that really counts." - John Wooden, UCLA basketball coach

"The greatest mistake you can make in life is constantly fearing that you will make one."

- Elbert Hubbard, American Writer

Leadership is a set up.

If you want to do meaningful work in a home office, you need a good set up. If you want to run a successful event, set up is what matters most. Designing success is the first step in achieving anything - especially when it comes to leadership.

The way that you set yourself up is what ensures your success.

Lots of books have been written about leadership: what it is, who is qualified for leadership, how to make hard decisions, etc.

In this book, I'm going to simplify what you need to know, so that you can do what needs to be done.

Transformational leadership is not a concept. It's not an idea, or an ideal. It's the most necessary thing in the world. And it can be simpler than you realize.

Let's set up for success - so that you and your team can excel, achieve, and grow.

I come from a military background. As you know, the United States military is focused on leadership. That's not necessarily how we are trained - it's more fundamental than that. Leadership is how the organization grows. Now, that "growth" comment may sound strange, because the US military is a shrinking force. But learning to do more with less is a key component of leadership.

While I was still a student at Texas A&M University, I was commissioned in the US Army as a second lieutenant. Over the course of my service, I was deployed in multiple combat zones, including Bosnia, Afghanistan and Iraq. During my career, I was fortunate to receive the Legion of Merit, the Bronze Star Medal with two oak leaf clusters, and the Purple Heart Medal. Later, I transitioned to the Texas Army National Guard, and retired with the rank of Brigadier General (brevetted).

But my leadership service was never about me. The recognition was like a ripple in a pond - it was what happened after we did what we needed to do. I understood what I needed to set up in order to succeed. And success was never the accolades or the titles. Success meant completion of the mission. I carried this understanding with me, as I earned my law degree and started my law practice, and as I moved into leadership in state government.

Understanding how to set up a winning team is what allowed me to turn around one of the most important agencies in Texas, the Texas Alcoholic Beverage Commission (TABC). But more on that in a moment.

As a military officer, they don't let you sit idle somewhere. You're constantly being measured. That's not to say that "Hurry up and wait" doesn't apply in the military. It does. But performance is what matters most. And, as a leader, you're being asked to evaluate your squad, your platoon, your team. It's always 50% up and 50% down - meaning, you have half of the folks that are making progress, and half that aren't. Move up or move out. Tough standards, right? But that approach creates a certain mentality - it builds a tendency towards action. And, when it comes to matters on the battlefield, it can truly be a matter of life and death. You want the best people in their roles, ready to perform.

The world of business is different, and I've come to understand those differences firsthand. Building and leading a team, without the benefit of rank and structure, was a challenge I readily accepted. And, through the challenges I have faced in my professional career, I've come to understand the principles that can set up your success. A rigid structure isn't required in order for you to lead. But you have to understand how to set up what you need - so that you can empower your team to achieve.

So, what action can you take, right now, to make sure that you are moving in the right direction? More importantly, what do you need to set up, so that your team can succeed? Whether you are leading a platoon of soldiers or a remote team of analysts, there's a common structure and approach that will form the foundation of your success. I call this foundational structure the First 90 Days.

The First 90 Days: A Template for Your Success

I took the reins at the Texas Alcoholic Beverage Commission

in the middle of a scandal. My predecessor had taken employees to a conference - which doesn't sound very controversial, now does it? But the conference happened to be in HawaiToi.

A statewide debate ensued, where the beaches of Hawaii provided a backdrop for allegations. Accusations of exotic trips and blended vacations showed a history of misuse of taxpayer money. A hearing was convened, by the Committee on General Investigating and Ethics, in the Texas House of Representatives. The net result was the resignation of the Director, as the agency was left in confusion and turmoil.

I came on board a sinking ship, where the first mates had just left, and the accusations of "misappropriation" had everyone on edge.

I needed a new set up. So, here's where I started:

ASSESS AND OBSERVE: 30 DAYS

I knew I needed to meet with each of the remaining 11 directors and find out about their challenges. That's when I made my first mistake.

I asked them what they needed.

In my experience, broad and general questions get broad and general answers. So, when I asked what people needed, I found out they needed a lot. At least, that was their perspective. They needed more money. They needed more people.

I asked the question before I had a real frame of reference - so I couldn't be specific. My team responded to me as if I were Santa Claus. Or a genie.

Step 1: Be specific in your questions, as you assess and evaluate.

It would have been better for me - and it will be better for you - to stay curious, before moving into questions about their needs. It's only natural to want to be of service, and asking what people need can offer some insight, but without context the conversation is too broad. You are not informed about what they are doing, so asking what they need is a question out of context.

Here are some better questions - what ideas do these questions spark for you?

1. What tasks has your department accomplished?
2. In what timeframe(s)? And how did those results line up with your objectives? (In other words, were they on track and on budget - or not?)
3. How many people were involved in that particular task? (Ask specific questions and get curious about the big objectives. How did the organization get that done?)
4. What resources did you use, to achieve that goal or accomplishment? (This question can help you to find out about existing systems, backchannels or bureaucracies. All of these things exist within every organization - get curious about what they look like in yours).

After connecting with the directors, I utilized a valuable and often-underrated tactic: MBWA. (That stands for management by walking around). Today, with remote teams, it's not always possible to have hallway conversations with people in an office. That shift just means that you have to be more deliberate about setting up a time to talk, and making sure you connect with everyone personally. Face to face or face to screen, it doesn't really matter. Stay curious and get specific about what you want to know. And resist the temptation to play Santa Claus.

In every organization, everybody is counting something. Maybe it's revenues, or profit, or inventory turns. As a leader, find out what people are counting.

And remember, just cause people are counting something doesn't mean that the numbers are valuable or useful. In my experience you can count on this: what is being measured may not always be meaningful.

At the TABC, the State Legislature was measuring how long it takes to get a permit to sell alcohol. If that number was high - meaning, the process was slow - community leaders and business owners were going to be calling their representatives. And then, the representatives would be calling the director (that would be me), and asking, "Why is our permit process so slow?"

As it turns out, slow permitting means a slower time to revenues. The entire economic engine, in bars and restaurants, comes to a screeching halt without the ability to sell to people - and alcoholic beverages are a big part of that equation. For example, in the city of Houston alone, there were 1,256 bars, 123 dance clubs, 17 beer gardens, eight country dance halls, 13 jazz and blues venues, 63 karaoke bars, 98 music venues, three piano bars and 52 pool halls. Bars and nightclubs across the State of Texas brought $2.4 billion to the state's economy - and that doesn't include restaurants that serve alcohol. Slow permits meant a slow economy - and slowing the economy slows down sales tax revenues for the state.

In the US, one of the primary goals is making money - but that's never the whole story. Profit and loss is always going to demand your focus, as a leader at any level. But there were deeper factors at play when I took over my role at TABC. Making money wasn't the full story, for the people on my team. Maybe what I saw is similar to what you are seeing, right now, in your organization.

Inside this unique state agency - a combination of policy enforcement and processing - there was a concept of family. In fact, it was more than just a concept for many employees - because their fathers and grandfathers had worked in the organization. There was a culture of family service, built by people who had literally worked in the agency for generations.

Were these people "in it for the money"?

Everyone everywhere wants to take pride in their work. We all want to feel like we are a part of something bigger than ourselves. And, yes, if that feeling is associated with "family" in an organization, that connection can be a powerful thing.

I observed that connection. I noticed the sense of pride in a job well done, inside the team. I saw that some people left the organization for more money. But the ones that remained had a sense of family. Whether it was part of their actual family history, or just an aspiration for a career dedicated to service, I knew I needed to step into the culture of the organization.

And that was when I was ready to move to Step 2.

STEP 2: IMPLEMENTATION
Identifying Gaps and Dealing with Hurricanes

The next thirty days had begun. It was time to move forward and start making some moves towards greater productivity. Once I met with the 11 directors, I discovered what was missing.

My team was too big.

Somebody - maybe even more than one somebody - wasn't going to get the attention they needed from me. I immediately set up three deputy roles. I used one person who had remained in the role and hired two others.

For me, I knew that I could effectively manage between three and five people. That's a little different than what you may have heard, especially if you are familiar with some of the theories of psychologist George Miller, or former Intel CEO Andy Grove.

In management circles, it's widely stated that the ideal number of direct reports is "7±2". That's seven, plus or minus two. The main idea here was put forward by Grove, in his book,

High Output Management. Widely regarded as one of the great leaders of the twentieth century, Grove says that leaders are expected to spend about an hour each week with each direct report. That's one hour with each of your chief lieutenants - considering the sum of all your interactions. That's between seven to nine hours each week, or about a fourth of your time (assuming a 40-hour work week).

Isn't it interesting the ideas that people put in books in 1995?

To be fair, Grove might have been on to something. George Miller, a researcher who is widely regarded as one of the founders of cognitive psychology, said that the limit of our human memory looks very similar: 7±2 items - in fact, in some circles, this statement is called "Millers' Law". However, since Miller came forward with his ideas (in 1956) we've shifted to 10-digit phone numbers. Not only that, we've also shifted to asking Siri to dial businesses and contacts from our phones.

As times have changed, we have to change. For me, I had always heard that 3-5 direct reports was the right way to go - and that's what felt right to me.

With 11 direct reports, I didn't do what Grove advised. I did what was on track for me. Because I knew I was going to need more time than what Andy Grove had theorized. I knew my needs and my limitations. Armed with knowledge, I arrived at a deeper understanding:

What the experts say is useful. But what works for you is what sets you up for success.

Step 3: Hold People Accountable to a New Standard.

From a place of respect, reflection and consideration, I set up the organization so that I could work best for my team.

But the organization was still out of balance. Two-thirds of the agency reported to one person - and that person had not been out in the field in the last five years. At that time, we had 48 field offices, across the largest state in the lower 48. That's a lot of territory to ignore. Not paying attention for five years was a mistake - and not a strategy I wished to continue. As I was assessing and evaluating this situation, I wondered: How is this person able to do their job? After all, if you're not out there and interacting with the people in various field offices, how can you be effective? If you've ever visited Texas, you know that El Paso, Dallas and Del Rio are very very different places.

I took a third of the agency and put it underneath my chief of staff. And then, I created a deputy of business operations to help improve licensing, tax collection and approvals. I shifted the numbers, so we could focus on what needed to be measured - and what needed to be done.

Understand the process, reshape the people - and create the set up that allows everyone to succeed. That's the third step. But first, let's take a look at a summary of ideas you can use, right now, to cover your first 60 days - then, we'll move to stage three, which is implementation.

60-Day Summary / Leadership Guidance

1. Ask specific questions. Ask about what people have done and what they are doing. See if you can discover what people value the most -it will be different for each person, but their values will come through. Get curious about the way people interact - or find out why they don't.

2. Look for the things that show a sense of pride. A sense of connection. A feeling that is the result of a job well done. People will want to tell you what's

wrong - make sure you get an understanding of
what's right.

3. Leadership is a promise delivered. So don't make any
   promises you can't keep. Gather information, assess
   and discover - that's where the leadership
   conversation begins.

4. Hunt for the numbers. Look for the data that is
   meaningful, and measured (and remember, they
   aren't always the same thing). Then, add your own
   assessment: what numbers need to be tracked? What
   are we missing that needs to be measured?

5. Size your team appropriately. Maybe you are
   comfortable with 7 direct reports - maybe not. When
   it comes to leadership, there's no "one size fits all"-
   like a golf swing, or the way you hold a pencil,
   approach your team in a way that feels right for you.

Now, let's take a look at stage three. But first, before I move
into the third month of your leadership journey, we're going to
have to deal with a hurricane.

In August 2017, the largest storm to ever hit the state of Texas
started pounding the Gulf Coast. Houston, the fourth largest city
in the nation, was at the epicenter. Millions of people were
displaced from their homes, from Corpus Christi to Beaumont.
The area affected was the size of the state of New Jersey. Hurricane Harvey brought a total of 60.5 inches of rain to Nederland,
Texas - a 1,000-year flood event. Nothing like it has ever
happened in modern history.

Harvey was a Category 4 storm, with 140 mph winds, the
punishing rain lasted six days - affecting 13 million people from
Texas to Louisiana. At its peak on September 1, 2017, one third of
Houston was under water.

I was staying at the bachelor's office quarters in Austin, when my phone rang. It was Steve McCraw, the head of the Texas Department of Public Safety. His voice was clipped and measured. "I need some of your agents."

The Department of Public Safety (DPS) is the largest law enforcement agency in the State. The TABC is the third largest. With hundreds of enforcement agents all across Texas, I was in a unique position to provide service to DPS. But that service wasn't on my 90-day plan. In retrospect, no one had planned on what happened when Harvey hit. Everyone in the law enforcement community knew that we needed to do something. But what, exactly?

"How many agents do you need?" I said.

McCraw's next words were crystal clear. "All of them," he said.

The coast was being crushed by the storm. The next day, we mobilized about 80% of our officers - it was everyone we could spare. We pulled people from all across the state, and sent them to the Gulf Coast.

But their fight was my fight, too. I took my chief law enforcement officer, and his deputy, and we went to the Coast. Houston was our final stop. We had visited other sites along the Gulf Coast and seen the devastation firsthand. We brought barbeque (and gratitude) to the teams who were working so diligently to save lives and protect property.

As a leader, the unexpected is going to happen. Expect it. Expect the unexpected. And rise to the occasion, when the unplanned shows up. If your team is going through something, then you're going through it, too. Share that you understand. Share that you see what they are up against. Go and try everything you can, to help those people that support you. Support them, especially during times of unplanned crisis. The plan can wait. Your people can't.

If your vision is just your vision, it doesn't mean much - you have to get the organization to buy into what you want to achieve. The key is helping people to achieve, so that you can share your vision. Make sure that you are connecting with your team and sharing in their challenges. Help others, and they will help you. That theme is at the center of servant leadership, as described in the classic essay by Robert K. Greenleaf.

Essentially, servant leadership focuses on the idea of prioritizing the greater good. Making sacrifices is part of the greater good. Just like making hard decisions; it's about putting the organization first. Providing strong support to employees has to be part of your 90-day plan. And beyond. Because, if you don't take care of your people, they will "take care" of you. And not in a good way!

Stewardship, as Greenleaf describes it, means leading by example. You have to commit to being a part of the struggle and the solution, with a commitment that is shown in your actions.

At Texas A&M University, home of the Fightin' Aggies, there are a set of six core values that every Aggie knows (https://tinyurl.com/creatingexcellence-1). Those values are written in bold letters, on the exterior of buildings in the center of campus. Words like "Integrity", "Excellence", "Respect", "Leadership" and "Loyalty" the foundational concepts that are at the heart of the university, and its students. But perhaps the greatest of these six concepts is the idea of *selfless service*. As one A&M student put it, "If I had to tell you about Aggie values in one sentence, I would simply ask the question, 'How can I be of service'?"

As you begin your leadership journey, begin with your values. Begin with selfless service.

STEP 3:   Implementation - and Why Everybody Loves a Winner

As you know, people want to be a part of a winning team.

That's why it's so important to understand where people are winning - and where you need them to win.

The first part of your 90-day plan is assessment. The second part is about planning - even when the unplanned happens. And you don't have to have a hurricane in order to see where people are struggling. Build a plan around your people and consider how to structure the organization so that you can meet the measurements that matter. Because the next step is helping people to win. That's called *implementation*.

Bureaucracies tend to grow stale. Within the matrix of the bureaucracy, people begin to build stories around advancement. "I can't get promoted to GS13" the rationale says, "unless I have two GS12's working for me." This line of thinking was misplaced ambition, and it was far too evident inside my organization. That was what surprised me the most - people wanted more, so that they could be seen as more important, and therefore ask for more money.

That's not to say that everyone was greedy, or selfish, about their careers. But there was a distinct difference between law enforcement inside a bureaucracy, and the inner workings of the military.

On the surface, I expected that there would be lots of similarities between organizations that have similar purposes (to protect and to serve). Both military and law enforcement have rank, and structure - external similarities that did not necessarily reveal the internal differences.

In a bureaucracy, tenure meant more than talent. "Joe's been here the longest," the line of reasoning began, "so it's his turn to be Captain." Or Lieutenant. Or Department Chair. Or whatever. In the military, it's more about performance - the best person for the job is the one that does the job. Of course, it might appear that is not always true, but the intention was more of a meritocracy (putting the best person in the role) instead of a bureau-cracy (rewarding longevity).

Adding to the complexity was the fact that I had a law enforcement organization of about 250 people, and 400 team members on the civilian side. So, what was the answer? When it came time to implement a plan, should it be a military meritoc-racy, or a big budget bureaucracy, or perhaps...something different?

When it comes to implementation, you have to understand that the past informs your decisions. But the past doesn't make your decisions for you. Or for your people.

Within the TABC, there was no common frame of reference for "leadership". There was no leadership development program. So, I had to build it. And I didn't build it alone.

From a place of collaboration comes a new creation. That's true for me, and for my experience. It's also true for every successful leadership initiative, in every successful organization. You have to have buy-in. You have to have people that want to be on the winning team. And you have to show people how to win.

If you don't have buy in, you get compliance. Compliance creates the status quo. I was leading an organization that had been marred by scandal, and now we were faced with the greatest natural disaster in my state's history. Compliance wasn't enough. Repeating the past wasn't going to help us to create the future. So, I wanted to make sure that I implemented a plan that pointed towards three aspects of organizational excellence:

1. **Taking care of people internally** - identifying the performers and achievers, regardless of the amount of time they had been with the organization
2. **Taking care of our external customers** - for us, that meant the residents of the state, especially those who

were looking to gain liquor licenses, as well as making sure that regulations were being followed in establishments that sold alcohol.

3. **Train people to the new standard** - holding people accountable is crucial, when it comes to implementation. The set up here is: make sure you let people know what you need. Make sure they understand that you are serious about your objectives, your goals and your measurements - and that they make these goals their own. People will either get on board - or they will go somewhere else. Either way, you win. And so does your team.

IMPLEMENTATION CAN BE SAID SIMPLY: "walking the walk". In other words, doing what you say you are going to do, and asking others to do the same.

Notice that word choice there: *asking*. Because you are seeking buy-in, not compliance.

Jack Stack, the author of *The Great Game of Business*, said it best: "People will support what they help to create.

If you see what you need done, if you see what the organization needs, there's a question you have to ask. You have to ask your team if they see it, too.

You have to ask your team if they share a commitment to a common goal.

You have to get that buy-in, and it's as simple as asking for an agreement. An agreement that allows others to say what they are going to do. And then, instead of giving orders, you're watching to see what people are doing right.

There's a school of thought that says that leadership is command and control. And there's another school of thought that says that command and control is dead. Well, once you've graduated from school, perhaps there's another way of looking at leadership. John Wooden said it best: "It's what you learn after you know it all that really counts."

Leadership is about helping your team to win. Gaining buy-in means you capture the hearts and minds of the people on your team. There's a shared purpose, because people identify that purpose on their own terms. People commit to objectives in their own words. People act in order to advance the mission - or they don't.

Either way, your 90-day plan allows you to continue seeing new possibilities. If others are not on board, you can course correct. You may not like the implications of confrontation, correction, or hiring and firing.

Some people don't like the alarm clock on their phones. But it always tells the truth. And the truth is, you have to make course corrections (and difficult decisions) when you are a leader. Creating excellence is about making those decisions in the right way - and helping others to do the same.

You can assess, evaluate and implement over the course of three months, or three minutes. Ask yourself these five key leadership questions:

1. From a place of selfless service, what does this organization need?
2. From a place of selfless service, what do you need from your team?
3. From a place of selfless service, what needs to be done?
4. From a place of selfless service, what needs to be measured?
5. From a place of selfless service, how can you encourage your team to win?

Control is an illusion. Can you control the weather, your

wife, or the wind? Of course not. But you have the power to influence. And you can put up the sail on your sailboat, or bring an umbrella, when circumstances come your way.

Leaders adapt. And that's not an isolated element on a punch list or a check box - you don't "adapt" on Thursdays at 2:30pm. You adapt all day, every day, and in every possible way. In every way that helps you to create the transformation you want, and the performance you deserve. Adaptability is what helps the team to win - and every human being is capable of making changes, when they see how your plan enables their success.

Create that vision for the organization. Build your plan with the input and buy-in of the team, so that you can help them to take ownership of the objectives that matter most. And gain that commitment - because that's when you know you are set up for success.

TAKE ACTION:
These exercises aim to provoke new thinking around the themes of the chapter, fostering collaboration, and empowering

team members to contribute to the organization's success. Each chapter in this book will provide you with prompts, so that you can turn the lessons from the chapter into actionable leadership results.

Are you ready to begin building your own 90 Day Plan? Curious about Creating Excellence, on your own terms?

Start here:

Reflect and Define Your Values

- **Action Prompt:** Take some time to reflect on your personal and professional values. What principles guide your decision-making? Write down three core values that you believe are crucial for effective leadership.
- **Exercise:** Share your values with your team and encourage them to do the same. Discuss how these values align with the organization's goals. Create a values statement that can serve as a guiding force for your team.

Assessment and Curiosity Exercise

- **Action Prompt:** Practice specific and curious questioning. When interacting with team members, ask questions that delve into their accomplishments, challenges, and aspirations.
- **Exercise:** Conduct one-on-one meetings with team members using specific questions provided in the chapter. Focus on understanding their achievements, obstacles faced, and their vision for the team. Use this information to tailor your leadership approach.

IDENTIFY MEANINGFUL METRICS

- **Action Prompt:** Identify key metrics that truly matter for your organization's success. What numbers should be tracked to align with the organization's objectives?
- **Exercise:** Collaborate with your team to determine the most meaningful metrics for success. Ensure that these metrics are aligned with both internal team goals and external customer satisfaction. Share the chosen metrics with the team for transparency and accountability.

SIZE YOUR TEAM APPROPRIATELY

- Action Prompt: Reflect on your preferred number of direct reports. How many individuals can you effectively manage while providing the necessary attention and support?
- Exercise: Discuss your preferred team size with your leadership team. Explore the reasons behind your choice and encourage an open conversation about team structure. Adapt the organization's structure to best fit the needs of the team and the goals of the organization.

LEADERSHIP BUY-IN AND AGREEMENT

- **Action Prompt:** Consider how you can gain buy-in from your team. How can you ensure that team members feel connected to the organization's mission and objectives?

- **Exercise:** Introduce the concept of buy-in during a team meeting. Ask team members to articulate their commitment to the organization's goals in their own words. Facilitate a discussion on shared purpose and encourage individuals to actively contribute to the mission.

Leadership is a process. And, like any process, it helps to have a system - a way to methodically approach the challenges inside your organization. What systems do you have in place, right now, to take you through the first 90 days - and beyond? And what do you do, when facing the unexpected? That story - and more - is ahead.

3

INSIDE ENEMY TERRITORY

"Your friends will believe in your potential. Your enemies will make you live up to it." - Tim Fargo, Founder of Omega Insurance and author of *Alphabet Success*

"In the practice of tolerance, one's enemy is the best teacher."
   - The Dalai Lama

They didn't want us there.

Inside Afghanistan, in the hills near Tora Bora, information didn't flow freely. In the months following 9/11, many of the people we were there to protect from the Taliban didn't understand why coalition soldiers were patrolling the streets. The Afghans I visited with didn't know about Bin Laden, or what he had done. They didn't know that the Twin Towers had been destroyed in a brutal terrorist attack. It goes without saying: on September 11, over 3,000 people were killed in New York City, the Pentagon, and in a field in rural Pennsylvania (where Flight 93 crashed after passengers overwhelmed the terrorists inside).

For many in Afghanistan, that story was unknown. They didn't know that the Taliban's refusal to turn over Bin Laden had led a global fighting force to occupy their country. They didn't know that the unimaginable cruelty and terrorism of Al-Qaeda had mobilized an international response from the US and its allies. For the locals, communication consisted of two threads: misinformation, and no information. In the hills and rural areas, armed soldiers from around the world were mobilized for reasons that had never been explained to the locals. All the Afghans knew was that, once again, an occupying army was in their country. Suspicion, speculation and misunderstanding: somewhere in there was our starting point.

Russia had occupied Afghanistan for 10 years, from 1979-1989. Now a new fighting force had arrived.

Same story, different soldiers? Not by a long shot.

Amanda Mason, Senior Curator for the Imperial War Museum in London, explained our presence in Afghanistan like this: "The leaders of Al-Qaeda have been based in Afghanistan since the 1990s, running training camps there. The American Government issued an ultimatum to the Taliban Government that ran Afghanistan at this time [after 9/11], demanding that they hand over all Al-Qaeda personnel still in the country and close the training camps." When the Taliban refused on every front, military action was next.

Efforts were successful in the early days. "American special forces liaised with and fought alongside anti-Taliban groups known as the Northern Alliance," Mason reports, "forcing the Taliban from their strongholds in Masari Sharif, Kandahar and Kabul. Despite a fierce battle in the Tora Bora mountains, bin Laden escaped capture and fled across the border into Pakistan."

With most of Al-Qaeda driven out of Afghanistan, bin Laden

gone, and the Taliban regime at an end, it might seem that the US had achieved most of their goals by late 2003. At this time, President Bush called for a period of "stability, stabilization and reconstruction activities."

But they didn't want us there.

And that's when I showed up.

How do you build trust within a culture that doesn't understand your presence? Perhaps what I learned at the table with the former Taliban and their allies can help you to enter into unfamiliar territory. Because you may not be in a war zone, but when you show up in a leadership role, there's one thing you have to understand: some people may not want you there.

Some may not understand what you hope to accomplish.

Some may doubt that you are there to help - especially the ones who prefer complacency over initiative. The Gallup organization explains it like this: imagine that your organization is a canoe, and there are 10 people in the canoe, each with their own oar. Two are rowing in the right direction, moving the canoe forward. Six are watching the scenery go by, and two more are actively trying to sink the boat.

Some may be in a zone of unknown - where a lack of communication has created suspicion and speculation.

You don't have to be in a remote rural area, in a hostile nation, to experience resistance, hostility and back-channel disruption. Leadership - and hostility - isn't something that's reserved for the military during times of crisis. Reluctance is always a given. That's why leadership is what is needed, right now, within your organization.

I share an experience with you from Afghanistan so that you may see the parallels - and the possibilities. As a leader, you have to see the common threads. The story of one of us just might be the story of all of us, if we are open to seeing the connection. Inside a mud hut or inside a multi-level industrial complex, you must recognize that leadership is not a matter of geography, experience, or structure. This is a book about leadership, and that means it's about you.

Your journey.

Your experience.

Your ability to see the commonality, even in uncommon circumstances.

In Afghanistan, I found myself in uncommon circumstances. I had to have tea with the Taliban.

I was there to run a civil affairs outpost - to help the commander win the hearts and minds of the Afghan people, so that we could all go home. And, on this day, our affairs were not in order. I knew what we needed to do. The question was, could we do it?

Inside a mud building, hundreds of kilometers from Kabul, in a remote area of eastern Afghanistan, I was part of a team that was conducting an investigation. A small security detail of four accompanied me to the meeting, all of us heavily armed. My team stood nearby - because no one and no thing in this office was more than four or five feet away. That included the soldiers guarding our host, who were also heavily armed. Near the wall that was opposite the entrance (there was no door) there was a small wood burning stove. Unprotected, the red embers inside offered little warmth against the cold Afghan winter. Beside the stove, there was a blanket, covered with large pillows. Our host greeted us, and we all sat down on the ground. In front of a platter of dried fruits and nuts, a compact man sat on the edge of the blanket, frowning and staring at me. Our host wore a traditional robe, the color of the desert sand. My meeting with the Village Elder had begun.

We met with the Elder, to share an important message - and clarify a deep misunderstanding. A tragedy had occurred, as tragedies always do in times of armed conflict. A group of children had been gunned down, and the word on the street was that the US military was responsible. The village had been used by Taliban forces - either they supported the Taliban, or (more likely) they went along with the Taliban because of threats or coercion.

I knew that we had not committed the assassinations. I could prove it, and I was here to try and fix it. I had to convey what we had learned. But first, I had to learn about *pashtunwali.*

Pashtunwali was the reason we were having tea in the middle of an investigation, in the middle of a war zone, in the middle of the mayor's office. Pashtunwali refers to the way of life in Southern Afghanistan, and indeed in any land where Pashtuns live. At the center of this cultural code of honor, unwritten but understood by all who follow, is a profound respect for all visitors. It is a kind of hospitality that must be shared, and displayed, for any and all guests. Even us.

Indeed, the hospitality of the Afghan people is well-known and well-documented. It is disrespectful for an Afghan to deny a guest food, shelter or protection. *The Nation*, Pakistan's national paper of record, describes Pashtunwali as a multi-faceted code of conduct, dealing with new visitors outside of pre-existing relationships or circumstances.

"'Melmastia' (hospitality) is a key component of Pashtunwali. "Melma" means a guest. However, hospitality is not to be interpreted in the manner a Westerner would interpret it. It means offering hospitality to a guest, transcending race, religion and economic status. It also means once under the roof of the host, a guest should neither be harmed nor surrendered to an enemy."

For our hosts, we were not only an invading army. They believed we were responsible for killing seven children. And we were also their guests. We were (they believed) a force to be tolerated, because eventually we would leave. So, they served us tea.

It was a little surreal. Imagine the scene, filled with soldiers and guards:

"How do you take your tea, sir?" "With my rifle on my lap, thank you."

Notice that hospitality is not agreement. Or acceptance. But it is a starting place for the conversation. Hospitality mattered to our hosts, and culture dictated that we honor and respect this tradition. We wanted to develop a relationship of trust and respect, and so we began.

But my mind was racing. This teatime could quickly turn into something much more dangerous, and I knew it. We were there to discuss a remedy - solving a problem that we knew was a consequence of someone else's actions. (In this case, it was our enemy - the Taliban). How could we take this incident to build trust, and gain support from the Afghan government, in a remote mountain village, far removed from the city of Kabul? How do you enter into enemy territory, to convey news that is different from what everyone believes? Was this meeting going to go sideways?

I wondered if I could build a bridge. If I shared a message of service, honesty, and truth, would it be received in the spirit I intended? Could this situation be fixed, or somehow resolved? I needed to go beyond hospitality. I had to. I needed to gain the Elder's trust.

How could I do that, when I had a story to share that was going to contradict their narrative? An Afghani doctor had blamed the US military for the deaths of seven children. What their doctor had said was not true. We were not at fault. But would they believe me? Or would they hide behind the lie that had become their narrative - that this invading army was responsible?

I noticed the village soldiers standing all around me. Their faces were wrapped so that only their eyes were visible. All eyes were on me, as we began the meeting.

Have you ever felt like you were an occupying force in a foreign country? Maybe you can understand what I was experiencing, maybe not. You know that feeling, when what you have to say is going to contradict what people believe, even though you know it's true?

When entering into a potentially hostile meeting, notice that there's something more important than courtesy, and hospitality.

It's *respect*.

I BEGAN by acknowledging their position. Respect is where leadership begins. Without respect, all the tea in the world isn't going to make any difference.

As best I could, I spoke through an interpreter about what they had heard from their doctor. I started with what they knew, so that I could introduce new facts.

New information would go beyond courtesy, to help create trust. At least, that was my intention. Step one was acknowledging their point of view.

Notice that acknowledgement is not agreement, either. Acknowledgment is understanding. Acknowledgment says, "I see where you are coming from."

That's not a position for manipulation, or a tactic for some kind of "gotcha!" moment.

Especially when you are in a room filled with guards, bullets and differing ideologies. An insincere and inauthentic approach isn't leadership - it's a recipe for disaster.

I began with understanding, as I spoke to the Village Elder about the significance of their loss. I shared our side of the story: I explained that someone from the Taliban had been using a satellite phone to call in false reports to London and other European news outlets. The spread of misinformation about the United States and our allies had to be stopped. The mayor understood, and he was listening. Our electronic surveillance picked up and traced the satellite signal, and an A10 Warthog was dispatched to the location of the surveillance. My interpreter explained the situation, and how that airplane was tracking an adult male in his thirties, using the satellite phone, near a stream that provided water to the village.

The A10 Warthog is a close-air support attack plane, known for exceptional maneuverability (if not high speed). Its frontal armament is a massive 30 MM cannon, called the GAU-8 Avenger. It's one of the most powerful mounted guns on any aircraft in the world. This massive weapon fires 65 rounds *per second*. A 30 MM round is rarely used against individuals; it's an armor piercing round used to penetrate buildings. Why? Because a 30MM shell used in the GAU A-8 cannon is bigger than a beer bottle.

To put it as delicately as I can: the target with the satellite phone was neutralized by the A10, including the building he was in.

But no children were harmed. We eliminated a threat; we did not kill children. And certainly not with 30MM shells - that made no sense. Who would order a strike from an A10 Warthog on children?

A doctor who examined the children said we did. He said the children were killed by shell fire from the A10. The Afghani doctor said we were responsible for the deaths.

Our investigation showed that the children - seven kids in all - were killed by small arms fire. We had documentation to prove it. In a separate and completely distinct incident, the massive weaponry of the A10 had eliminated the satellite phone threat. But there was no collateral damage from that mission, no attack on children. The events were unrelated. I shared with the village elder that - although the US was not responsible for the incident - we understood the tremendous loss to the village. We wanted to help our friends, the villagers.

In any armed conflict, cruelty and casualties are a part of the picture. But we had to give the village elder a clearer picture than the one he had. And that's what we did.

The Taliban, the former governing body of Afghanistan, had massacred a group of children, so that they could pin that story on the US military. That's what the enemy - our mutual enemy - did.

WHILE THERE'S no amount of money that can replace a child, we wanted to compensate the village for their loss. We wanted to build trust and take steps to make an offer that would somehow build a bridge. We wanted them to understand that we were not the bad guys in this situation. That part of the conversation was another layer of diplomacy - a delicate and nuanced message.

I was ready to negotiate the compensation package, when Lieutenant Tony Alvarez stepped forward and tapped me on the shoulder. Tony pulled me back. Told me to wait.

I PAUSED.

Our conversation had gone out into the courtyard, an area in between buildings that was separated from the prying eyes of the village. There, we were walking and talking - interpreters, local officials, heavily armed guards and my soldiers. One of the village elders had joined our conversation and was walking ahead of me with his hands clasped behind his back. He wore a *chapan* (coat) of thick fabric, to protect from the chill of the Afghan winter. Although I couldn't see his face, I noticed the back of his turban, or *lungee,* as he nodded and spoke. Beside him was one of my sergeants, dressed very differently, but matching the elder's posture and pace exactly. The sergeant walked with his hands clasped behind his back, listening and talking...and building a relationship based on trust. Alvarez, after he saw that I was not going to intervene, clasped his hands behind his back, and stepped forward to rejoin their conversation.

Alvarez saw what I had missed, and he joined my sergeant in deep discussion. These three men were negotiating, developing a relationship based on mutual respect and agreement. It was not time for me to take the lead. Or was it?

At that moment, leadership was listening. Patience was the action I needed most. So I waited, thanks to my lieutenant, Alvarez, who pointed out what was going on. I stepped back. I let the elder, Alvarez and my sergeant finish what needed to be said. Why?

Because leadership is about timing.

And knowing when to let others take the lead.

Those NCOs (non-commissioned officers) had been doing that job for years - tackling tough conversations and brokering deals inside of Afghanistan. My job was to facilitate them, to continue to let them do their job, not tell them how to do it differently. I know a lot of lieutenants who struggle with this idea - the idea of letting others take the lead. Because they come out of the basic course thinking, "I know everything there is, you know, because I'm an officer."

Well, maybe you are an officer, and a leader, but you don't know what kind of leader you are. Other than someone who won't let experts do their job.

If you think leadership is about being the hero in every story, you're missing the point. Sometimes the action you need most is facilitation. The mission is more important than the person who completes it. What can you do, right now, to help your team to win?

Sometimes you don't have the luxury of evaluation and reflection. You have to decide, right now. The choice is dictated by outside forces. Many times, we must move forward with imperfect (or incomplete) knowledge. Leadership is about making tough decisions, like knowing when to act. And when to step back.

Sometimes leading means, you have to practice "five finger management." Are you familiar with this concept?

You take five fingers, like you have on your left hand. And you take all five of those fingers, and you use them to cover your mouth. Is it impossible for you to speak now? Congratulations. You have achieved five finger management. And it needs to be in every leader's repertoire. Because sometimes what you don't say is more important than what you do.

Especially if someone on your team is more experienced than you are. Especially if you see one of your sergeants demonstrating a greater cultural knowledge than you possess. Whoever told you that you have to have all the answers? Leaders create teams, they don't try to be the team.

"Leaps of greatness require the combined problem-solving ability of people who trust each other...Leadership is not about being in charge. It's about taking care of those in your charge." - from Leaders Eat Last *by Simon Sinek*

Inside the mission, we find meaning. We do what we need to do, in order to achieve the objective. Not to receive personal notoriety. The team has to win; you have to get past self-serving accolades. Lead by letting others take the lead. Let your team step to the forefront. You don't have to solve every puzzle or captain every conversation.

When I started my new role at the TABC, I wanted to know who was really on my team. I wanted to know who was watching my back - or if I was in enemy territory. Remember, resistance always exists when any new leader arrives. I'm not instructing you to be suspicious, I'm encouraging you to be informed. Knowing this fact, I held a meeting with my entire team.

Remember the line from President Reagan? "The nine most terrifying words in the English language are, 'I'm from the government. And I'm here to help.'" I wondered if I was living inside that punch line, as I started my role in Austin.

I had taken the job at TABC because the organization needed to be transformed. How did I get there? Well, my predecessor had walked into a standard review conversation with some state legislators. Supposedly it was a warning, or simple "slap on the wrist", for some recent spending choices. She went in with her guard down. She was ambushed - confronted with a searing analysis of her past actions. Could she have defended her choices better, in that setting? Perhaps. Would it have made a difference? There's no way to know. But what we do know is: no one on her team warned her. Somebody had to know that the ambush was coming, didn't they? Someone could have told her. But no one did.

Her intel was missing. She had a simple plan for a simple meeting, and the plan was incomplete. Did the members of her team withhold information? Did they "hang her out to dry", in a confrontation with legislators? The unexpected attack led to her demise, and resignation in disgrace from the position. I knew I couldn't put myself in the same situation. I needed better intel.

So, I started by looking at the character of my employees.

"Why would any of you," I began, "want to work for the state?" I paused to let that one sink in.

Maybe they thought the question was rhetorical. Or crazy. Maybe they thought that my appointment wasn't going to last. Maybe they thought they would just "wait it out". Have you ever had a team that took a "wait and see" approach?

The conference room was filled with all of my direct reports, seated at a large u-shaped table.

"There's a perception that people have when they think about state employees. Is that who you are? Because that's not what I wanna be," I said.

Yes, it's true: I have been employed by the government for much of my career. However, the military is more of a meritocracy than a bureaucracy. Because, in the military, an officer is either up - or out.

So, for this new team, I wanted to know if they were going to be "typical" state employees. If they were going to hide behind bureaucracy, hide behind vital intelligence, hide behind the status quo.... or step forward and support what I needed them to do. Complacency was not going to help anyone.

I didn't have time to wait. I had my mission, and now it was our mission. As a government employee myself, I knew deep down that most government employees are hardworking people. They are trying to do the right thing. I wanted to know that I didn't have a faction of disruptors, or folks that wanted to retire at their desks in the middle of their careers. We had been asked to do something important - asked by the Governor of the State. And I needed their help to get it done. A "typical" government attitude wasn't going to work. I wasn't being suspicious. I was curious - curious about how we were going to work together. Was I in enemy territory? I needed to know.

There are always obstacles to change. I'll elaborate more on those obstacles in the coming chapters, as well as offering strategies so you surround yourself with the right people. But for now, suffice it to say, you have to get buy-in on the mission. You have to make sure that the people you are supporting are supporting you.

Look at the team that surrounds you. Do you have good people? Then let them do their job. Get out of the way. And if you don't have good people around you, it might be time to change the team. Notice that leadership grows when you give it away. You don't have to be in a remote Middle Eastern village, or recovering from a statewide scandal, in order to see that.

Recognize that you don't have to go it alone. Look at the people that surround you. Curious about their character? Ask them. And if you find yourself inside a team built on trust (as I did at the TABC), don't cut off their skills. Instead, offer support to them - and they will support you in return.

That support was what appeared on that cold December day in Afghanistan, as we walked through the dusty courtyard outside of the village meeting room. The elder, Alvarez and the sergeant did what I wasn't ready to do. They brokered the compensation. They built a bridge. They created trust within the culture of *pashtunwali.* And we were all better for it.

Did I lack the initiative or the intelligence to broker that courtyard deal? Was I somehow ineffective, and that's why I stepped back? Could the village elder and I come to some agreement, at some point, in the future?

I have a single answer for all of those questions; *Who cares?*

None of these questions matter whatsoever. Speculation like this is a spiral that has no end and no beginning. Speculation is self-serving. That's not leadership.

Instead of these questions, here's a better one:

Did we accomplish the mission?

Yes. Yes, we did. On this day, everybody won.

Getting it done isn't always about the who, or the how. Follow the rules, respect the boundaries, and color within the lines - but get it done.

Leaders know that there are many paths to the same destination. Finding a way to win means finding *every* way to win.

If you come into a situation thinking you know what the problem is, and you don't bother to "take a walk", you might miss something. Without the space for assessment, without that tap on the shoulder from a trusted advisor, without asking some hard questions, you may be fixing something that isn't broken. You might keep running your mouth instead of recognizing a solution. You might rush in, when patience is what's needed.

And by the way, do you know who will always rush in? Fools. Fools rush in.

Suspicion is not satisfaction; that's no way to run an organization. The mission is what matters most. Keep your eye on the ball.

It's hard to do that if you're looking in the mirror and asking, "What if...?"

Leaders assess. Leaders step back. Leaders ask hard questions. And leaders listen. Leaders aren't afraid of five finger management. Because, when you really understand leadership, you live this principle: it's not about you.

TAKE ACTION:
Leadership in Unfamiliar Territory

- Reflect on a situation where you felt like an outsider or faced resistance in a professional context. What strategies did you use to build trust and understanding? If you haven't faced such a situation, imagine a scenario where you are entering a new team or organization that is initially resistant to your presence. Outline the steps you would take to establish trust and navigate the unfamiliar territory.

CULTURAL SENSITIVITY AND EFFECTIVE COMMUNICATION

- Think about a time when you had to convey a message that contradicted existing beliefs or narratives. How did you approach the situation to ensure your message was received positively?
- Consider the cultural context, the emotions involved, and the potential impact of your communication. What strategies can you apply in your current or future leadership roles to communicate effectively in diverse and potentially resistant environments?

RECOGNIZING AND LEVERAGING TEAM EXPERTISE

- Assess your current team or a team you've worked with in the past. Identify individuals who possess specialized knowledge or expertise. Reflect on instances where you allowed others to take the lead based on their expertise and describe the outcomes.

- If you haven't had such an experience, consider a hypothetical scenario where you need to rely on a team member's expertise. Outline how you would facilitate and support their leadership in that situation.

FIVE FINGER MANAGEMENT EXERCISE

- Recall a situation where you refrained from expressing your thoughts or opinions during a team discussion or decision-making process. What was the outcome, and how did your restraint contribute to the team's success?
- If you haven't consciously practiced "five finger management," consider a scenario where silence or restraint might be more impactful than speaking up. Describe how you would apply this concept in a leadership setting.

BUILDING BUY-IN FOR A MISSION:

- Analyze the team or organization you are currently a part of. Evaluate the level of buy-in for the overarching mission or goals. If there are signs of resistance or complacency, outline strategies you would employ to build stronger commitment and enthusiasm for the mission.
- If you are in a leadership role, consider how you can effectively communicate the importance of the mission and foster a sense of shared responsibility among team members?

4

FINDING TRUST

"Few things can help an individual more than to place responsibility on them, and to let them know that you trust them." - Booker T. Washington, US Educator, Reformer and African American leader

"Better to trust the man who is frequently in error than the one who is never in doubt." - Eric Sevareid, CBS News War Correspondent, 1939-1977

Trust takes time.

In the small towns of Afghanistan, shortly after 9/11, people lived in mud huts, receiving water every other day. In the remote village where the elder lived, the only generator in town was for the mosque. Kabul - the center for government - had little influence in the countryside. Because there was really nothing the government could do for them, or to them, these people were beyond influence. After all, what do you take away from someone who has a dirt floor in their living room, and the water won't arrive until Tuesday? The standard of living was hard to imagine, unless you saw it firsthand. And, when I did, I realized that these people had nothing left to lose.

In order to build trust, we had to walk a mile in the other guy's shoes - or sandals, as the case may be. For us, leadership wasn't about carrots and sticks (reward and punishment). Leadership was about understanding. Understanding another person's perspective and building trust.

David Horsager, author of *The Trust Edge*, says that the number one question that everyone is asking is, "Can I trust you?" (https://tinyurl.com/creatingexcellence-3) And when he says everyone, he means all of us. Inside any organization, everyone wants to know if the leader is trustworthy. Credible. A person of integrity.

In his runaway best-seller, Horsager defines eight key pillars of trust. But the one that stood out for me was the idea of *character*. In other words, trust begins with who you are. Horsager writes:

Character: *People notice those who do what is right ahead of what is easy.* Leaders who have built this pillar consistently do what needs to be done when it needs to be done, whether they feel like doing it or not. It is the work of life to do what is right rather than what is easy.

IT'S BEEN SAID that integrity is doing what's right, even when no one is looking. As a leader, it's a good idea to consider that someone is always looking. Even if that "someone" is you.

Considering Character: Building Trust

How can you know the character of anyone?

How can you, as a leader, assess the character of others - and inspire your team that you are a person who keeps their word? It's counter-intuitive, but the way you establish character isn't by talking about your accomplishments or past history. That story might *describe* your character. But the way others experience your character comes from the way you treat them.

The way you treat people starts with the way you treat yourself. If you don't hold yourself accountable, you can't hold others accountable. You can't create excellence if you don't expect it from yourself.

My favorite way to figure out what's going on in an organization is to walk around and talk to people. And if you've got a remote organization, you've got to set up a time to talk. No agenda, other than a conversation, is the key. All you need to bring to the conversation is a sincere curiosity.

And when you set up that conversation, just remember people will withhold things.

That is, until you walk a mile in their shoes.

One of the elders in the village would invite us over for tea and conversation. In Afghanistan, the tea is served hot, and sweet. You could say how much sugar you wanted, but it was coming to you sweet.

Except at the mayor's office.

He was stingy with his sugar.

Did he have sugar? Yes. Yes, he did. But, unlike some other local leaders, he chose to portion it out in small quantities. I never understood why, exactly, until I remembered human nature.

People are going to withhold things.

Like the weather, withholding doesn't always make sense. But it always exists.

Trust opens up the conversation. Even when the sugar supply is closed off.

Management by walking around, or MBWA, isn't about wandering aimlessly, or asking people about the weather and where their kids go to school. I'm not saying that kind of small talk and connection isn't important. But leaders go deeper. And leaders know that observation is the key to leadership.

That means, seeing, understanding and experiencing what your team is really up against. Otherwise, you're leading from assumptions, rather than firsthand confirmations. Have you walked a mile in the other person's shoes?

It's one thing to call someone into your office and ask them to open up about the challenges that they are facing. But, if you do that, remember: people withhold things. Especially when they think that they are being interviewed, or interrogated. Or they might think you've got a hidden agenda. If you call someone into your office, they may imagine that bad news is waiting for them.

A better leadership strategy is to catch them doing something right.

Walk into their world.

Go see their cubicle, their operating environment.

Imagine this scenario: someone under your leadership comes to you and says that they are having a challenge with a particular aspect of their job. Do you fully understand what that challenge is, and why it is an obstacle? Have you seen what they face, and do you truly understand it from a firsthand perspective?

"I've served with lots of officers," Kean Register says, "and General Nettles is the only one who's gone out with me on patrol." One of my former NCO's (noncommissioned officers - someone who supervises the enlisted soldiers), Kean is a natural storyteller with a quick smile. In addition to a distinguished career in the Texas Army National Guard and then U.S. Army Reserve, he served as a city manager for seven years in the community where I live.

Kean and I would go on patrol together. We'd be bouncing around inside a helicopter at night, checking out different landing scenarios - trying to figure out if a particular site was suitable for troop deployment, or maneuvers, or whatever the mission might require. But I wasn't checking those landing sites on a map, sitting behind my desk. I was in Sergeant Kean's world, and able to see what he saw, and did. Why is that perspective vital?

When I ran the Texas Alcoholic Beverage Commission, I went on sting operations with my law enforcement officers. Our mission was simple to describe, but difficult to do. Our agency was there to regulate the alcoholic beverage industry, to make it safe for residents of our state. Within every aspect of our operation, I asked myself: how do we do that (create safety and ease of doing business)? How are we working together, in fulfillment of that mission?

Underage drinking, or consumption, is against the law. And overconsumption (being over-served, public intoxication, drunk driving, and more) leads to multiple risks and legal consequences - dangers that we all know. We know that alcohol can be a source of fun, connection and enjoyment - or a destructive force when it's abused, misused, or sold inappropriately.

Setting Up the Sting

There would be a team of four law enforcement officers, going out in the evenings, to look for violations at bars and restaurants. Typically, they operated in two person teams, with one team entering the establishment undercover, wearing plain clothes and the other team would be outside. There would also be a supervisor either outside or available by phone if more than one group of officers working in the area. Two of the officers would be "open". That's another way of saying they were openly identified as TABC agents.

These officers were not dressed in your typical police uniform, but they did have a sort of uniform that made them "open". At the request of business owners, and by order of the State, our officers were not necessarily a visible patrolling force. A more casual approach was chosen for our attire, so as to be less disruptive to the place of business, and to the public, for our agency.

Both open agents wore a simple black polo shirt with the agency logo on it. That night, the agents both wore a badge on her belt. They carried the standard issue Glock 19 firearm on their thick black belts, and tan colored canvas cargo pants. The supervisor spoke first, as he adjusted his wireframe glasses. "Here's what we are looking for tonight," he said, making sure that the young girl with blonde hair could hear everything.

The agents employed operatives, like this teenage girl, to pose as customers in bars and restaurants. The agents used both men and women who fit a certain profile: they had to be no older than 19 years old. The men had to be clean shaven. The women did not dress provocatively. The operatives were actors, in a way, and they had to be able to perform their parts: ordering drinks and showing their actual IDs to servers, doormen and restaurant managers.

Seems simple, right? Especially in the State of Texas, where people under the age of 21 are all assigned a special kind of driver's license for identification. (Several other states also have a different shape for underage drivers - including New York, Indiana, Idaho, Michigan and more). Under 21 gets a vertical ID, so a portrait shape makes it easy to see which adults are under the legal drinking age. For adults over the age of 21, the license is horizontal - displayed in a landscape view.

In a sting operation, the operative will go into an eating or drinking establishment with the undercover officers within sight. The agents are able to see and overhear what is being said, when drink orders are placed. The supervisor and I were outside the establishment, so as not to cause suspicion from the establishment employees.

In a setting like this, it's important to have eyes and ears on the situation. If laws are broken, the restaurant might try to lay claim to a different version of the facts. Or a bartender, who sold drinks to a minor, doesn't want to tell the whole story.

We were there to get the whole story. We were there to observe.

As a leader, are you taking time to make sure you are observing? Watching? Discovering the challenges that your team is facing? Do you have the whole story?

GETTING OUT IN THE FIELD, talking with your employees and observing their tasks is a great way to see what needs to be done.

In Texas, making alcoholic beverages available to a minor is a class A misdemeanor, punishable by a fine up to $4,000, confinement in jail for up to a year, or both. Your drivers license would also be automatically suspended for 180 days when you are convicted of selling alcohol to a minor. All that to say, if you work in the restaurant industry: don't do it. Because, if you do sell alcohol to a minor, it is the server (not the restaurant) who is immediately liable (https://tinyurl.com/creatingexcellence-4). You don't want the hassle, and you don't want that mark on your record.

This kind of sting operation - this kind of enforcement - was the tip of the spear for the TABC. I needed to understand what they were doing. And on that night, the blonde operative flashed her state issued portrait ID and ordered a cocktail. When the bartender served her a drink, an unfortunate scene began to unfold.

Seeing the service of the alcohol, the undercover agent excused herself and went out to the parking lot. She sent in the two open agents, and they served a citation on the spot to the server who had brought the drinks. My supervisor and I sat in the booth. We watched as surprise, disappointment and regret moved across the server's face.

The server was confronted by two TABC officers and given a citation. The manager was notified, and the employee was dismissed for the evening. The supervisor later told me that sometimes things can get thorny, but tonight's incident was a smooth one. Ultimately, charges will be brought and handled through local law enforcement channels.

The role of the TABC agents is inspection, so that agency-licensed businesses are kept within regulations. The role of the leader is an inspection of sorts, as well. Inspecting and observing what your employees are facing, every day. Look for people doing something right. Look for the obstacles that keep the right things from happening.

As a leader, you have to be the one to step into their world (instead of inviting them to sit down in yours). That way, people are not as threatened, and they will begin to open up to you. Asking someone to come into your office can immediately create unwanted suspicion: "Uh oh", your employee wonders, "what did I do wrong?"

The scene changes completely when you go to their world.

You see what they are doing, and what challenges they face - and your observations drive the conversation. You aren't dealing with some prior agenda, unnecessary suspicions, a past report or prior dashboard review. You're seeing what's happening, in real time.

Your ability to observe, and your ability to serve, is key. "Going on Patrol" isn't something that's reserved for officers in state agencies, or for my friend, Kean, in the Texas National Guard. Meet your people where they are. Show up with a spirit of curiosity, and service.

Ask about what challenges they are facing - not in some broad, general, MBA-textbook kind of way. But based on what you see, inside their foxhole (or their design meetings, or from across the aisle at the restaurant, or inside the lines of software code, or as you observe their architectural drawings). Meet your team where they are. And observe.

The key to establishing trust is to get outside of yourself. Conversations are useful. Observations are invaluable. And sometimes, when you really need to see what's going on, you have to hide your bars.

Maybe you remember the scene in *Band of Brothers*, where Major Winters (played by the brilliant Damian Lewis) is leading the liberation of Eindhoven. Winters and Lieutenant Welsh (Rick Warden) are seen tucking their bars - the insignia that displays their rank - into their collars. (https://tinyurl.com/creatingexcellence-5) Lt. Compton, played by Neal McDonough says, "What's up?", referencing the decision to hide the symbols of their military status. "Snipers", comes the reply. Compton gets wise, and he hides his rank by doing the exact same thing.

Have you ever considered how status or rank might work against you, with your team?

In a battlefield situation, snipers often target military commanders in an effort to disrupt the chain of command. Taking out the leader can create disarray - cutting off the "head of the snake", so to speak - by targeting the highest-ranking members on patrol. Many situations are "no salute" zones - where signs of respect can put an unwanted target on your back, if observed by the enemy.

When you go on patrol, you go as equals. That's true in *Band of Brothers*, and it's true for leaders who value character. Are you on equal footing with those you lead? Are you able to walk a mile in their shoes?

Maybe you don't face snipers and sharpshooters, literally. But there are those who are on the lookout for leaders who rely on rank, instead of service, in order to lead.

The power of a leader comes from what you can do for the team, and for the organization. Not the title on your business card, or the bars on your collar.

Later in the series, near the end of the war, a new lieutenant shows up and wants to lead a second patrol. The episode, called *The Last Patrol*, is a powerful lesson about leadership. The "new guy" picks the wrong team to go out on patrol. But he's in charge, so he makes the decision. He makes the call. He makes the mistake.

Colin Hanks, playing Lieutenant Jones, wants to lead a patrol into battle before the end of the war. "But the decision was not up to him," the narrator says, pointing to the fact that cooler heads prevailed. That second patrol was never sent - saving the lives of the men and resulting in promotions for many. For Lewis' character, he is surprised by a black box that's tossed to him after the mission is completed.

"Oak leaves" he says, simply, opening the box. An award of

valor, and recognition of achievement - because of what the platoon had done. The team had achieved something, and the leader was recognized. In my experience, that's how it works.

For leaders, notice that sometimes it's the action not taken that yields the result that's needed. The discernment to know what's needed is how leaders establish trust. And character.

As the episode ends, the narrator asks, "How can anyone ever know of the price paid by soldiers, in terror, agony and bloodshed, if they'd never been to places like Normandy, Bastone or Hagenau?" (Or from this generation, we might ask about Kabul, Helman province, Fallujah and Baghdad?)

The story of Easy Company, as told in Band of Brothers, is a moving depiction of real events. The series depicts a commitment that most of us, today, can only understand via movies and books.

The character of the men and women who fought in World War II is something I often consider and admire. We all stand on the shoulders of those who have gone before us. We enjoy the lifestyle we have today because of those who have fought for our freedom. That commitment points to character, and service. And it reminds all of us - in every kind of career - that we are capable of so much more than we realize.

We don't have to storm the beaches of Normandy in order to show our character.

"CHARACTER IS how you treat people who can't do anything for you in return. Integrity is how you act when you think nobody is looking."

— Nelson Mandela, President of South Africa 1994-1999

THE BATTLES we fight now are battles for greater understanding -

building bridges and creating trust, so that we can solve the problems of today, and tomorrow.

When I went on patrol with Kean, I had to hide my bars. When I went on the sting operation, I went as a participant, not as someone in charge. I had to learn what others were doing, by observation, so that I could help them to see new solutions. I hid my rank without hesitation - especially when Kean and I went out into the night, to observe, to learn and to serve.

When I went on patrol, I didn't have all the answers. In fact, I was made of questions.

Get Out from Behind the Dashboard: See Beyond the Screen

If you are managing and directing based on what you see on a dashboard, how can you be truly effective? How can you take into consideration the character and the concerns of the people you serve? Without that firsthand understanding, you are flying blind. If you are leading by the numbers, and you don't know what it takes to generate those numbers, what kind of a leader are you going to be?

Leaders have to be comfortable with not knowing all the information. That's not an admission of guilt, or weakness. That statement is the gateway to curiosity. After all, what are you guilty of? Being human? Not having the experience of your entire team? That's a good thing - if you stay curious. If you observe. If you become more informed, and lead from a place that includes people above the process. But this has to be done in balance. You are still the leader, you still have to make the call, even when you have imperfect knowledge. You have to be confident in the call and ensure your subordinates are confident in you making the call. I think asking questions and learning about the challenges faced by the employees and the organization will make you a better leader.

When I was put in charge of the TABC, the third largest law enforcement agency with state-wide jurisdiction, I didn't technically have a law enforcement background.

But I had a leadership background. What do you think matters most?

Creating excellence comes from understanding what really matters, when you are given an assignment. If you're passionate about leadership, about leading organizations to excellence, then you can lead any organization to excellence. Don't get lost in the details of your past experience, your shortcomings, or even your own characteristics.

If you're looking at yourself, you're not looking in the direction of leadership. Want to know how the leader is doing? Look at how the team is doing. Are people engaged? Are people supported? Are people staying with the organization, and holding one another accountable?

These are the characteristics of true leadership - a leadership that empowers. A leadership that is focused on what matters: service to the team and the organization.

Help other individuals to be great, and the organization will succeed. Make success your expertise, and you will create excellence.

Widgets, gadgets, platoons or state agencies...Organizations exist to perform functions. Notice that, within the nuances of business and service, there is functionality. Figure out what the functionality is, and you are on your way to creating excellence.

What are the tasks here? How do you apply resources to that task in the most effective manner? How do you grow the organization by developing the team - so that the team becomes more than its individual parts?

Nobody expects you to know everything. Unless you put that

pressure on yourself. Look, I appreciate high standards, and I'd like to think I have them. But set a standard that's useful. Set a standard of understanding. As Stephen Covey said in *The 7 Habits of Highly Effective People*, (https://tinyurl.com/creatingex cellence-6) "seek first to understand, then to be understood".

It's counter-intuitive, but your credibility as a leader is based, in large part, on your ability to observe, understand and appreciate your team. Your success depends on them, just as their success depends on you. Trust begins when you step into their world, with no agenda other than understanding.

One of the fastest ways to get thrown out of my office in Austin was for an employee to say, "That's the way we've always done things."

Quoting chapter and verse from yesterday's news is no way to build the future.

Why do we do things that way, I want to know? I would tell folks that they can come back and see me when they are ready to answer that question. Why would someone let the past dictate the future? We always have the capacity to change, especially if that change is in our best interest.

Maybe there's a really relevant, fresh and current reason why we do things the way we do. If so, I'm sincerely interested in hearing it - and learning more!

But if the best reason you've got is, "Well, that's how some senator wanted it done 20 years ago," I wonder if you are even listening to yourself? Would you use a cell phone from 20 years ago? Arguing for the status quo is not a wise leadership position.

Reexamine things. Never be afraid to ask why. Creating excellence begins with curiosity. A curiosity that says, could we do this better?

As a leader, lean into the expertise of your people. But let your expertise be in the area of curiosity. Aren't you interested in doing things in the most efficient way? Inquire what that way might be. Otherwise, you're going to be eating a sandwich stuffed with the status quo.

I've had people serve it to me, and that's a pretty stale sandwich. I always send it back.

In my campaign for public office, I've closed more than a few speeches with this message: "I know that you're wondering whether or not you can trust me. I'll simply say that for 32 years, the American people, and the people of Texas, have trusted me with the most valued asset: their sons and their daughters. I think you can trust me with your vote."

It's true that people withhold things. But when they see your character - and they see that you understand their world - new possibilities come into play.

Trust takes time. But leaders look in the direction of acceleration.

Growth.

Possibility.

Can you say these words to your team, with confidence and clarity? These simple sentences are the first steps in finding trust:

- **I've walked a mile in your shoes**
- **I've seen what you are facing**
- **I don't know - but I'm here to find out**
- **Let's go "on patrol" together**

Creating excellence requires trust, and time. Meet people where they are and let them know that you're not here to fight for the status quo. Neither should they.

There's a bigger and more important battle ahead, and you're going to need everyone's support to get there.

TAKE ACTION

"Walk in Their Shoes" Challenge

o   **Exercise:** Identify a team member or colleague facing challenges in their role. Arrange a one-on-one meeting with them to discuss their experiences, obstacles, and goals.

o   **Guidance:** Actively listen and seek to understand their perspective without judgment. Ask open-ended questions and avoid jumping to solutions. This exercise is about gaining first-hand insights into their world.

"Observation Leadership" Task

o   **Exercise:** Spend a day or part of a day observing different teams or departments within your organization. Aim to understand their daily operations, challenges, and successes.

o   **Guidance:** Take notes on what you observe and use this information to inform your leadership decisions. Look beyond data on a screen and embrace the opportunity to connect with your team on a personal and operational level.

"Challenge the Status Quo" Initiative

o   **Exercise:** Encourage your team to question existing processes and norms. Create a forum for open discussions where team members can propose improvements or alternatives to current practices.

o   **Guidance:** Emphasize the importance of innovation and improvement. Be open to new ideas and ensure that team members feel supported in challenging the status quo for the betterment of the organization.

"Leadership Patrol" Experience

o   **Exercise:** Schedule time to shadow a team member in their daily tasks or projects. Experience their work environment and witness firsthand the challenges they encounter.

o   **Guidance:** Act as an observer, allowing the team member to lead the experience. Ask questions and seek to understand the intricacies of their role. This exercise fosters a sense of camaraderie and demonstrates your commitment to understanding their work.

"Curiosity Leadership" Mindset

o   **Exercise:** Acknowledge and embrace the phrase "I don't know." Encourage a culture of curiosity within your team, where admitting uncertainty is seen as an opportunity to learn.

o   **Guidance:** Lead by example by expressing curiosity about different aspects of the organization. Encourage team members to seek understanding before making assumptions, fostering a culture of continuous learning and improvement.

5

A SURPRISE ATTACK

"Rapidity is the essence of war: take advantage of the enemy's unreadiness, make your way by unexpected routes, and attack unguarded spots." — Sun Tzu, The Art of War

"If you do not expect the unexpected, you will not recognize it when it arrives." — Heraclitus, Greek Philosopher c. 500 BCE

There is no such thing as complete information. Leaders everywhere are forced to make decisions with imperfect information, because if they wait too long the decision is no longer relevant.

The unexpected surrounds us. Surprises are everywhere. So how can you prepare for the unexpected?

The best answer I can give you is you can't. Not completely, anyway. Because if you are completely and totally prepared for the unexpected, then it's not really unexpected, is it?

Four words that can make a powerful difference for you, as a leader, are the following:

I've thought this through.

To the best of your ability, it's important to assess risks, gather information, and pool your resources. The key for the leader, in creating excellence inside uncertainty, is insight.

An insight into the nature of surprises, challenges and unexpected opportunities.

That insight is: complete information does not exist. Not for you, not for me. Not for anyone.

Not even ChatGPT has complete information. That may sound hard to believe, because it's digested 100 million books, or more, as well as countless bits and bytes of other information.

Yet its output, like your output and mine, maintains a certain level of unpredictability.

And there's one thing that ChatGPT will never know or understand, and that is our specific human experience. The things that make you the unique leader that you are - these traits are part of your character, not necessarily your LinkedIn profile. (By the way, ChatGPT has already read that. Or it soon will).

Look, this isn't a chapter about AI, or a book about new technology. The point I'm trying to make here is: we have to be comfortable with uncertainty.

We have to use the tools and resources and ideas that we have, so that we can think things through. But if you think you will make decisions with complete information, think again.

Consider the handling of the COVID crisis in Texas - perhaps the greatest surprise attack in our lifetimes. Any way you look at it, the pandemic was a surprise attack. Did Texas "get it right", when it comes to the handling of the crisis? Did any of us "get it right" during the pandemic?

Let's set that issue to the side. And I'll leave it to you to take sides. The point here is to say - and share - how options appeared, and how decisions were made. Those decisions were made with incomplete information, throughout the pandemic.

What can we learn, as leaders, to help us in creating excellence - inside a surprise attack?

The State of Texas began tracking COVID-19 outbreaks by counties, during the pandemic. Business came to a standstill - but Texas is a pro-business state, and Governor Abbott knew that re-opening was the key to keeping the economic engine humming. Consider that, if Texas were a country, it would be the eighth largest economy in the world. (https://tinyurl.com/creatingexcellence-7)That's right - Texas would be ahead of Australia, Italy, Mexico, Russia and Spain. Greg Abbott had a huge responsibility - a huge decision to make. Would keeping businesses open expose customers and workers to life-threatening illness? Or was it necessary - because, without the flow of goods and services, people would also be negatively impacted.

A decision needed to be reached - a decision that somehow balanced the need for economic prosperity and health considerations.

The decision looked like this: once you get below a certain level of COVID outbreaks, each county can decide if they're going to reopen the businesses. Allowing each county in Texas to make its own decisions was important, because of the diverse geography and size of Texas.

Consider, for example, Rockwall County. Rockwall is the smallest county in the state, with only 149 square miles. That's less than half the size of the city of Fort Worth, or about the same size as the tiny Isle of Wight in the English Channel. Meanwhile, out in west Texas, Brewster County is the home of Big Bend National Park. That county - the largest in the State - has over 6, 180 square miles. That's 23% larger than the state of Connecticut.

Consider what happens if you shut down the largest employer in any county, large or small, and those people go home. They can't work. There is no work. They're not getting paid, especially if they're hourly workers. While it's true that the government programs at the time provided relief and compensation, access to that relief takes time. And, for some families, a subsidy check in the mail wasn't enough.

Thanks to the Governor, county leaders were trying to reopen the Texas economy as quickly as they could. Leaders were making decisions that they believed to be in the best interest of the people and the state. And, economically, Texas was able to survive and even thrive during the pandemic.

Did they make the right decision? That's the wrong question to ask.

What did they do, to make the decision right? What did the people in the counties, and across the state, do to create excellence?

Texas employment levels, according to the Bureau of Labor Statistics, fell by 11.2% between February and April 2020. As you know, March 13, 2020, was widely regarded as the day the earth stood still, at least across the United States. In November 2021, 21 months later, Texas employment levels reached pre-pandemic highs. Compare that rebound to the recession of 2008, brought about by the Global Financial Crisis. That recovery took 39 months.

Consider what happens when you shut down businesses: you can potentially wipe out somebody's livelihood. You destroy their 20-year savings in their business that they had just opened.

Yes, you kept 'em alive. But at what cost? And at what quality of life? How do you balance that?

It is always the toughest decision any leader has to make, balancing between two equally important forces. Welcome to leadership: choosing between options that can result in undesirable consequences. COVID isn't the only example of complexity in decision-making. But beyond the data, where is the insight?

As you consider the leadership decisions you are trying to make right now, I don't know what you are facing. But I do know this: you're dealing with imperfect data all the way around.

So, what's the answer?

The answer lies in insight and understanding.

Understanding that the answers have to come from inside of you, even in extraordinarily difficult decisions. Making a choice with incomplete information is often the best that we can do. No leader has complete information - and every leader has felt what you are feeling, right now. As the saying goes, "Heavy is the head that wears the crown." That's not to say that you are a queen or a king, or that you must be a royal in order to feel the weight of leadership. Difficult decisions are the burden of all leaders, everywhere.

Making a tough call means following up, to make the decision work.

Want to make the right decision? Then work to make the decision right. To find excellence inside of the unexpected. To empower your team to get comfortable inside the unknown. And to abandon unrealistic expectations of how much data you need, in order to move forward.

Sometimes the greatest gift you can give your team is the gift of understanding. Understanding how decisions are made, so that they can make their own decisions.

After all, if leadership is a gift (and it is a gift), consider carefully how you can give it away. How you can add understanding and insights to your own self-leadership - but also, how you can share this wisdom with others.

Because the unexpected always exists. Take the information you have and make a good call. And if you realize the call is wrong, back up. Reassess, and go forward again. Stop looking for a template, or a "paint-by-numbers" way to do things. What others have done can inform, but the ultimate decision rests with you.

Inside any situation, second chances always exist. Even if it's just a chance to show up differently, inside the exact same situation. Indeed, "new beginnings are often disguised as painful endings," according to Lao Tzu.

Maybe you can't go back to your ex-husband or have a second chance at that State Championship. But you can show up differently, for new relationships. And you always have a chance to do what Lou Holtz told his players at Notre Dame: "Play like a champion today."

The game may change, but your intention towards excellence remains the same.

Leading through change means showing up differently and making a new decision. "Your present circumstances don't determine where you can go. They merely determine where you start," according to university founder, Nido Qubein.

Here are some powerful leadership questions, inside of difficult decisions:

1. *What needs to be done?*
2. *What can we do, to balance two challenges or differing points of view?*
3. *What can we do to make this right?*
4. *What are you going to do, to make this right?*

As a leader, you will have to make tough decisions. Consider the viewpoints of others, gather wise counsel, take in a variety of viewpoints if you can. But ultimately, deciding is about making a choice.

Choose wisely. But don't wait. Because decisions are opportunities for learning. And decisions can change.

Assael Romanelli, a clinical social worker and licensed therapist in Israel, writes in *Psychology Today*, "When babies learn how to walk, their parents cheer them on with every misstep. They do not criticize them or give them the 'feedback sandwich'—they just clap. When we start learning how to walk in this world, we're not making mistakes but rather we are experimenting and exploring. Whether our choice is right or wrong—there are no mistakes.

As we grow older, we become scared of getting it wrong, of failing, of being ridiculed. So we shy away from mistakes. We try to control everything; we try to be perfect, and that perfectionism is actually a form of self-blocking from creativity."

Romanelli ends with a troubling outcome from trying to be perfect: "We stop experimenting and growing."

Keep growing. Keep pursuing growth for your team and your entire organization. Keep experimenting. Because experiments never fail.

If you have an idea that's formulated in your mind, as it takes shape, move forward like a scientist. Treat your idea like an experiment. You are testing your hypothesis.

The scientist, after running an experiment, is always better informed - regardless of the outcome. Can you run some experiments, on your own, right now?

What is your hypothesis that begs to be tested?

"Wait!" I can hear you saying, "what about that COVID example you just gave? What if I'm making a decision that's a matter of life or death?"

My first question is: Is it? Is your decision really a matter of life and death? Or does it just feel like people might die, if you make the wrong choice?

There's nothing wrong with caring so much or feeling so deeply. But dealing with reality is much more useful, from a leadership perspective. You've got to see things as they are. Don't get lost in the way you feel about your circumstances, your team or even yourself. Put your attention on what needs to be done, not hyperbole (exaggeration) around your situation.

Jeffrey Hayzlett, author of *Running the Gauntlet* and founder of the C-Suite Network, dials decisions into a business context. He says that leadership is serious business, "[Often] while lives are not at stake, livelihoods are. If you are not successful, jobs will be lost. Mortgages and retirement and college funds will be affected. This is not a game. Driving change is about driving success and is serious."

Acting scared - which is another way to describe inaction, freezing up, and embracing mediocrity - is not the answer. According to Hayzlett. "You don't ever *know* what's going to work. One mistake or setback does not mean total failure. Seven of every ten things change agents do will be good and three will fall flat. Those are good odds." He closes with a reminder that, in the world of business, when we make decisions, *no one is going to die*. (https://tinyurl.com/creatingexcellence-9)

We assign an importance to choices (as well we should, if we care about our organizations and our teams). How much importance are you assigning to your decisions? To the decisions of your team? What happens if you access what scientists know: that detachment towards the outcome helps you to stay better informed, and more aware, of what the experiment is trying to teach you?

Can you help your team and your people to see that making things better is the experiment we all need to run? Fearlessly, and with detachment from the outcome, we ask ourselves, what could we do better? Creating excellence begins with this question. Setbacks happen when you are leading an organization. But so does learning. Learning is how we grow as individuals, and how we grow our teams.

Inside the classic book, *Blue Ocean Strategy*, written by INSEAD professors W. Chan Kim and Renee Mauborgne, they advocate finding calm waters even in the midst of chaos. Blue oceans, in the book, are represented by those calm waters. The "blue ocean" means all the industries not in existence today - outside of the "red oceans" of churn, turmoil and existing competition.

So, what do these colorful ocean metaphors have to do with creating excellence? Ultimately, finding the blue ocean strategy is about differentiation and competitive advantage. But a blue ocean exists inside of decision-making as well - if you are able to see it.

Harvard Business Review says, "In blue oceans, demand is created rather than fought over."

Look outside of the fight, the chaos, and the turmoil to find new solutions. To run new experiments. Discover new demands - from your customers, your team, your constituents. Seek out the blue ocean: discover the uncharted calm waters, in terms of solutions and leading through change. As Edison said, "There is a way to do it better. Find it."

In the blue ocean strategy, "There is ample opportunity for growth that is both profitable and rapid." But growth and opportunity don't just appear inside a metaphorical ocean. Conceptualizing leadership can be useful, up to a point. Then it's time to get down to business and get going.

Ultimately, the blue ocean strategy is about altering the boundaries of an existing industry. What are you doing, as a leader, to alter the boundaries of a challenge or obstacle? If you are wondering what establishes the boundaries of a challenge or obstacle, the answer is always the same:

It's the way we think about the situation.

The way we view a circumstance determines how we approach it. Like the person learning to snorkel, in a pool, and he suddenly begins to hyperventilate. Gripped with fear, he's terrified that he can't breathe! Something is wrong - he feels like she is going to drown, as water has gone into his snorkel and into his mouth.

Quickly, the instructor approaches the flailing student. Outside of the student's duress, the instructor offers a quick reminder. Namely, he gives a nudge. The student, on the verge of drowning, stands up. He's out of the water, and he catches his breath.

Because he was standing in three feet of water.

Do you think you're drowning in the shallow end? Does someone on your team need a reminder, that "no one dies", as Jeffrey Hayzlett has said in *Running the Gauntlet*?

It's useful to remember it's never tougher than it is in your mind.

In many ways, life is like a word problem, if you remember those days from math class. I've got two boys in high school right now, and the one thing I always tell them is: the way you set up the problem determines how you solve it. Most word problems are really pretty simple, on the arithmetic side. Look, I'm no mathematician, but helping people to set up a problem will determine how they solve it. How *you* solve it, as well.

Here are two useful leadership questions, when facing adversity, challenge and unexpected change:

1. *What else could this be?*
2. *What else could this mean?*

These two questions point you away from the status quo, and away from preconceptions.

The antidote to preconceptions is possibility.

Exploring possibility begins with stepping back and looking at things in a new way.

When it comes to decision-making, how are you altering the boundaries of the existing challenge? How are you stepping back, and seeing things that others don't, or won't, or can't?

This perspective is critical, so that you can find the "calm waters" of new possibilities. They're out there, even if you don't see them at first.

There are two ways to create blue oceans. In a few cases, companies can give rise to completely new industries, as eBay did with the online auction industry. But in most cases, a blue ocean is created from within a red ocean when a company alters the boundaries of an existing industry.

The right way forward is always an experiment. An opportunity to learn. A chance to make a choice. And making that choice right, through your actions. Especially when those actions involve stepping back, taking a fresh look, and deciding on a new course of action. Remember that, in most decisions, no one is going to die.

But what about when we are faced with matters of life and death?

For me, I faced death.

Just before I took a shower.

See, I was going to go for a run on this particular morning. But the Sergeant Major at the base had just put in new speed bumps on all the roads across the base. But the speed bumps hadn't been painted. I wasn't going to go for a run in the dark, and risk turning my ankle on an unpainted obstacle I couldn't see. So I headed for the showers instead, to start my day.

A day that was far from what I expected.

The shower trailer is exactly like what you would imagine: a mobile home that has been converted into a place where you can shower. Divided in the middle, there were three sinks on each side. The other half of the trailer was shower stalls. The two rows were separated by a wooden bench in the center, where you could sit down.

In Freedom Village, inside Camp Victory in Baghdad, privacy was at a premium - even for a Lieutenant Colonel in the wee small hours of the morning. It was just before 4am when I hung up my robe and started brushing my teeth.

Even at that hour, another guy came in while I was putting away my toothpaste. I didn't really notice him, after he came in - I was focused on getting my own act together. I headed for the shower, in my t-shirt and shorts, when I realized that I left something on the sink.

So, I walked back towards the entryway, headed for the sink. That was when the rocket hit.

It was a 120 mm Katyusha rocket. This type of rocket was first built by the Soviet Union in World War II. The word, Katyusha, would be translated as "Katie" in English. Comrade Katie packed quite a punch, especially when that shell hit just outside the shower trailer.

The explosion was deafening - quite literally. I still have hearing damage from the blast to this day. I was knocked down by the impact. The lights went out. Disoriented, I heard the blast of steam from the water heater that had been pierced in the calamity. I got up and moved towards the door, trying to find my footing. I called out to the stranger who had come in after me. I called out again, but - ears ringing - I didn't hear any response.

I got outside, walked down the short stairs from the trailer, and sat on a bench. I put my hand to my forehead. I pulled my hand back from my head wound. That was when I felt the blood dripping into my eyes.

Imagine the scene.

The smoke.

The wreckage.

The base was alive with activity, trying to take counter-measures and make sure that no more shells were on their way. A guy came by with a bandage, maybe he was a medic, I don't know, but he put pressure on my wound. I told him to check on the guy in the trailer, so he went in to check on him.

Other people came out of the trailer. But that guy - the guy that came in right after me - he never did.

He was dead.

I had narrowly escaped an untimely ending in my story. Meanwhile, a Chaplain (he was from Guam, but I can't remember his name) came to talk to me, as I sat there on the steps, bandaged and bloody. "You want to go to the clinic?" he asked me.

Seemed like a good idea. I went and put some clothes on and went to see the doctor. An Army reservist plastic surgeon happened to be on staff. He took the shrapnel out of the left-hand side of my body and stitched up my head wound.

All this time my ears were ringing, after the loud blast. The hearing loss would show up later. At that moment, I was grateful to be alive.

The other guy wasn't so lucky. God was somehow protecting me, on that day. It was a surprise attack. By the grace of God, I survived.

This was the first time I had served in Iraq. I had 12 members of my team, spread out across three separate commands. Three doors down from one of my guys, another rocket had hit. The trailer caught fire. One of my team members was knocked out by the blast and his door was locked. No one could get to him in the blaze. They couldn't reach him in time. He was consumed by the fire.

There are no "front lines" in modern warfare.

The front lines have been replaced with surprise attacks.

And with the reach and velocity of modern artillery, a sense of safety is...elusive, to say the least.

I came back from Iraq, during my second tour, for the birth of my first son. When I returned to the Middle East, the US position had been fortified. Walls had been built inside Sadr City, and the bad guys had been pushed back far enough that they were not shooting rockets at General Petraeus's headquarters anymore.

But surprise attacks don't just happen inside walled cities. Or outside an army base.

How, you may wonder, can you move forward and take action, when surprise attacks can happen at any time? Inside a place and a space that cannot be made safe, what can you do?

I don't know if I have the exact answer to that question.

But I will tell you what I did, after I got stitched up and dismissed by the clinic.

I went back to work.

I carried on, to set an example for my team.

I wasn't safe before the attack, and I wasn't safe now. Surprise attacks could happen at any time.

But there was something that was more important than concern, worry or fear. And that was my people.

If I was intimidated, the bad guys won.

If I stopped, the bad guys won.

I didn't want the bad guys to win, and I still don't. I wanted to return to duty.

Don't let the competition beat you. Don't beat yourself, before you get into the game. Awareness and action, these are the tools of the leader.

Firemen sometimes wear t-shirts that say, "We fight what you fear". I'm not a big fan of the self-congratulation in that message, but there's some truth inside the bravado. Really what they are trying to say, I think, is that saving you is more important than me. And isn't that the definition of selfless service? A sense of duty and purpose that overcomes the concerns of the individual.

Courage is really just selfless service - leaving yourself behind, and focusing on what needs to be done. Even if that means you need to go into a burning building, for example.

While you may not be fighting fires, or heavy arms fire on your way to the shower, consider the part of the story that's yours.

How important is your mission? Your team? Whether you are making widgets, or healing the sick, or teaching a room full of nine-year-olds, the real question is: how much do you care?

When we care enough, we look past the fear. We care enough to concentrate on what matters. Mission first, people always.

We see that surprise attacks can come at any time. (That's what makes the attack a surprise). We see that, in the midst of the unexpected, we can be resourceful. That resourcefulness is inside all of us - it's a human characteristic, like having opposable thumbs.

When we see that we don't have to be overcome with emotion, we realize that our thoughts don't have to derail our leadership initiatives.

Because we can feel whatever it is that we are feeling and still do what needs to be done. That's true for you, me, and human beings everywhere.

That capability - the ability to act in spite of our thinking - is a simple matter of focus.

Inside that focus is a consistent, measured, and steady drumbeat: a commitment to the mission.

The way you do one thing, as I have said, is the way you do everything.

Consider your goals, and your mission, and what you would

like to accomplish. As a leader, you have goals and expectations of your team.

Your future goals in this present moment are seen in your *values*. A surprise attack can happen at any time. Be ready by knowing what matters most.

What do you value? What does your team value? How are you helping people to recognize their values, and see their values in action? Because, without action, values are just concepts. It's like someone saying, "I value being on time," but showing up late (or not at all) for important events. What does that say about that person's values? What does it say about your values, as a leader, if you tolerate that behavior?

If you expect others to trust you, and entrust you with leadership, remember: make the promises that you can keep. Start by keeping promises to yourself. Start by living your values.

Explore how you see your values expressed in everyday life.

How do your actions and your values align? Ask that same question of your team members. Ask for commitment. Ask for people to show up for the mission.

There's a quote from Alan Watts, the English philosopher, who asks about the size of the sun. "Are we going to define the sun as limited by the extent of its fire?" he says. "That's one possible definition. But we could equally well define the sphere of the sun by the extent of its light."

What's the size of your leadership, I wonder? Maybe take a look at how you are sharing your own light, your gifts, and your insights. Notice how you, like the sun, radiate a commitment to the mission.

Because that commitment is how you survive - and thrive - in the middle of a surprise attack.

OPPOSITE PAGE, **Top:** Headed back to Iraq. I got home two days before my wife was induced and went back when our oldest son was 13 days old. My wife has always been there for me. Reflecting on those days, Tracy says, "Service means doing your job, even at great personal sacrifice for you and your family. It means walking into battle, being willing to lay down your life if necessary." I am truly a very lucky man to have her in my life.

OPPOSITE PAGE, **Bottom:** In Afghanistan, at the holidays, in the Tora Bora Mountain Range.

ABOVE: The ceremony for the Purple Heart, one of 24 awards and badges I received over the course of 32 years of military service.

My family will always be my greatest joy and my highest accomplishment.

Left to Right: Kevin Lily, Chairman of TABC, Texas Governor Greg Abbott, and me.

Left to Right: Lily, Texas Lieutenant Governor Dan Patrick, and me.

With Tracy by my side, serving local communities.

Leadership, then and now. Below: with Chancellor John Sharp, Texas A&M University.

6

STRATEGIC ALLIANCES

UNVEILING THE POWER OF TEAM DYNAMICS

"We don't accomplish anything in this world alone... whatever happens is the result of the whole tapestry of one's life... all the weavings of individual threads form one to another that creates something." - Sandra Day O'Connor, First Female Supreme Court Justice

"Coming together is a beginning. Keeping together is progress. Working together is success." - Henry Ford, American industrialist

The entire state of Texas was facing a huge challenge. Crimes were being committed, often inside of bars, strip clubs and other similar establishments. Lives were in jeopardy; people were going missing. A criminal enterprise was not only ruining lives. These criminals were taking lives as well.

Human trafficking was - and is - a major problem across the USA. Although the TABC had 250 Texas peace officers on our payroll, their day-to-day focus was on the enforcement of alcohol laws and keeping criminal activity out of permitted locations (places where alcohol was served and sold). We knew human trafficking was a problem. The governor asked for our help. What could we do?

To attack this statewide problem, I knew that the first thing we had to do was to train our agents to work undercover, in human trafficking situations. The TABC developed the first of its kind human-trafficking undercover school.

In the process, here's what we discovered:

Human trafficking is modern-day slavery.

Victims of human trafficking can be young children. Teenagers. Men and women. They can be US citizens, or foreign nationals. And these victims can be found in big cities, small towns, and rural areas.

The National Human Trafficking hotline has one of the most extensive data sets on the issue of human trafficking in the United States. Since 2007, the Human Trafficking Hotline (a combination of calls, online reports, email, texts and web chats) has identified 82, 301 cases of human trafficking. Nearly 165, 000 victims were identified in these cases.

WHAT ABOUT THE victims who were not identified?

The US Department of State recognizes an estimated 27.6 million human trafficking victims worldwide at any given time. That's more than the population of Los Angeles, New York City, Chicago, Houston, Philadelphia and the entire state of Michigan combined. There are more victims of human trafficking world-wide than there are people living in Australia.

In Texas, the border with Mexico stretches for over 1,250 miles. Inside this expanse, the opportunity for human traf-ficking was enormous. Women were being captured in Mexico, or lured under false pretenses, then turned to a life of prostitution and forced drug addiction.

As the state's alcohol regulatory authority, TABC takes the lead on any investigations of serious crimes, including human trafficking, at licensed businesses such as bars, convenience stores, and nightclubs. The agency partners with other federal, state, and local law enforcement agencies to investigate suspected trafficking and is a member of multiple anti-human trafficking task forces. (If you are curious to learn more about human trafficking efforts in Texas, check out the TABC page here.)

Problems are solved by people, when it comes to a global challenge like human trafficking. But did we have the right people? Did we have enough people? And did we have the resources (and the appetite) to fight this battle?

True, the Texas Alcoholic Beverage Commission is the third-largest law enforcement agency in the State, with statewide jurisdiction. But the challenges of human trafficking seemed enormous, the impact on lives severe, the humanitarian impact unimaginable.

We knew we didn't have the intelligence capability or resources to really assess where human trafficking was occurring within our state. At the same time, we knew that horrible crimes were occurring in our industry - in and around establishments where alcohol was sold.

According to the US Department of Health and Human Services, human trafficking can occur in a variety of situations. Strip clubs, bars, and restaurants are some of the places where this despicable act can take place.

Although our agents or auditors typically enter hundreds of retail establishments a day, we have constrained time and resources to do the regulatory work. Trying to identify and investigate human trafficking was an additional duty which the agency was not initially given additional resources to combat. We might go into an establishment on Tuesday, but the working girls didn't show up until Saturday. We needed someone who could regularly enter the establishment without drawing suspicion. While we didn't have the staff to go into all of these establishments, we found people who did.

BEER DISTRIBUTORS.

Through arrangements with major liquor distribution companies across the state, we got a message to hundreds (if not thousands) of key people inside the alcohol distribution business. Specifically, we talked to the folks who were delivering beer. The beer truck drivers became our eyes and ears, entering unnoticed into establishments where questionable activity was happening on a regular basis.

OPINION

'Beer drivers' are now being enlisted in the fight against sex trafficking

TABC is setting the pace for beverage commissions throughout the country.

Source: @TexasABC on X

Because the beer truck drivers go into these places - bars, strip clubs, and restaurants - daily. They go in, sight unseen, with an ease of access that is unmatched.

If we could reach these drivers, and educate them on the indications of human trafficking, we just might have a shot at mobilizing a "boots on the ground" task force. We could provide this mobile and highly present group of delivery drivers with an easy way to report into our agency. Then, based on initial information they provided, we could send in our agents and our auditors to check.

Not only that, but we also turned to survivors of human trafficking to develop the curriculum, and to train our agents. Our undercover school, for human trafficking, was the first of its kind in the US. Survivors were our professors. The training came from people who had lived through the horrors of this terrible crime. With new knowledge for our agents, and a mobilized surveillance force of delivery drivers, we were fighting the battle - and winning.

The entire operation became a huge success. Why? Because we offered education and training. And we discovered a new and untapped resource that was more than willing to help. In the end, we were asking these drivers to observe and report. Our training offered an additional layer of awareness, and we told them what to notice. We leveraged a segment of the industry to help in the fight against one of the cruelest and most reprehensible criminal enterprises in the world.

How are you using untapped resources to expand your reach? How are you training your team - and your extended network - to know what to notice?

The good book says, "As you seek, so shall you find." Are you mobilizing resources to expand your reach, and your influence? If those words matter to you, make sure you take time to train people. Show them what to look for and show them what you need. Especially if it looks like something "extra" - something outside of the normal scope of business.

Some in your organization may argue that "it's not in my job description" to do something new, or expand their duties. But creating excellence means remembering that job #1 is to get the job done. And the people – the team – is how it gets done.

If a statewide law enforcement agency can find new flexibility and adapt to new duties, your organization can do so as well. It's your job to help your team to see that the job description is simpler than they might realize. The job is to get the job done. Period. Helping people to see why new initiatives matter is the leader's priority. Capture the hearts and minds of your team, and you will see them take ownership (and action) on new initiatives.

At the El Condor Pool Hall in north Houston, we received reports of narcotics being sold on the premises (one of the warning flags we had shared in our training). More importantly, at least from the standpoint of our regulatory duties, alcohol was being sold after hours. Investigating these violations led us to work with multiple agencies, including the Department of Homeland Security, as well as local law enforcement.

The Feds took over and began to lead the investigation - but they got sidetracked. TABC stepped into the lead on the task force. At TABC, we carry dual authority - both criminal, and administrative. So, violations of code, as well as criminal violations, fell under our purview.

The joint efforts led to the arrest of 11 people on drug-related charges, including the owner of the liquor permit (the owner of the club). Our teams interviewed 19 women as part of an ongoing investigation into alleged human trafficking. Several grams of narcotics, including cocaine and heroin, were seized on the scene. The bar was shut down, its liquor license revoked immediately.

At a press conference in San Antonio, I joined the Fire Marshal and local law enforcement officials to discuss the disruption of a major human trafficking ring in Bexar County. I spoke of the work that was done with a 16 year-old female. She was both the main victim and the lead witness in the case. "We want to send a message to those criminals out there that think that they can bring juveniles and use them in this way," I said, "to take our children and put them in employment in strip clubs and businesses and our permitted locations [with liquor licenses]. We want to say, 'You're not welcome here, we're going to find you, and we're going to put you out of business'.

"There are 54,000 permitted locations in the State of Texas," I continued, speaking from the podium and addressing the cameras, during the press release event. Surrounded by police officers from Bexar County, we prepared to take questions from the room full of reporters.

"The majority of [business owners with liquor licenses] are good people. They want to comply with the rules of the alcoholic beverage code, which is a fairly complex code and law, and we try to help them with that. But there are those, and it seems that it's about 5%, who don't want to follow the rules. They want to treat their businesses like saloons in the Old West Days, and they do everything they can [to avoid the law]. That's illegal. We're going to make cases against them, and we are going to put them out of the alcoholic beverage industry in Texas."

The liquor laws were a gateway to resolving greater crimes and eliminating criminal activity. Our work to defeat human trafficking was possible because we had the right people in place. And the law was on our side.

Our administrative authority allows the TABC to go into any permitted establishment - any place with a liquor license - without a requirement for identification. We have the authority to do undercover operations, and to compel businesses to open their books for our agents. That authority and service, in permitted establishments, is part of our charter.

The location in question in this incident was called Club MGM in San Antonio. Here, an underaged girl had been forced into prostitution as part of a human trafficking scheme. The police department partnered with multiple agencies, based on her eyewitness accounts, to shut down the establishment.

You may be wondering why law enforcement partnered with the Fire Marshal, and the TABC, in order to close the club. The violations of the liquor license, combined with violations of the fire code, allowed us to close the business. And the testimony of the 16-year-old female led us to investigate several other locations that she had identified as sites of numerous infractions and felonies. The police arrested the owner of the club, brought charges surrounding employment harmful to a minor (also called "endangered employment"), prostitution and narcotics. This case led to the closing of another establishment, Blush, and ongoing criminal charges.

We were making progress. Our initiatives were beginning to show results.

We experienced a 700% increase in the number of human trafficking reports to our agency, in a one-year period. Of course, that kind of enormous increase presented its own level of challenges. But we made the reports a priority, and so did the alcohol companies who agreed to help us.

Because of our progress, the Wholesale Beer Distributors of America encouraged other states to enact a program similar to ours. Today, at least 12 states (that I know of) have engaged in new checks and balances, so that human trafficking can be stopped. It all starts with the beer trucks - it all starts with the drivers.

The key to finding the right people is giving them the right training. More importantly, creating the right kind of culture so that people can thrive - even people who are not necessarily a direct part of your workforce. Finding the right people isn't just about hiring. It's about finding the right partners, programs and providers. Then, serving your customers (or, in my case, constituents) in a way that's helping everyone involved in the process.

Remember: your customers, your constituents and your connections are all part of a larger ecosystem. If you're wondering if you've got the right people, I've got a better question for you.

Do you have the right communication?

Are you providing the kind of environment that helps people to succeed? As a leader, you know that you can make decisions to put the right people in the right seats. Or, as I learned in the military, to move some people up while moving others out. The challenge, for the leader, is to create an environment - a culture - that is clear. The right people need the right communication. Communication around expectations, empowerment and accountability.

Otherwise, you are going to have a revolving door where employees are leaving your organization - erasing longevity and shaking the foundations of continuity within your organization. You may say that "everyone is replaceable "but I would argue that culture is not. High turnover is not the mark of creating excellence.

Other books will tell you how to assess employees, evaluate résumés, and test for competency.

My concern here is your competency, as a leader. And that competency begins with communication. Here's how to communicate in a way that's more than competent - it's compelling:

1. **Set Clear Objectives:** serving under General William Petraeus in Iraq, I learned a few things about leadership. Petraeus outlines four steps to strategic leadership, including "Developing the Big Ideas", "Overseeing Their Implementation" and "Revising

and institutionalizing the Big Ideas". But the most important step is *communicating those ideas effectively.* Big Ideas alone are never enough. Enrollment comes from communication, and engagement - getting others to buy into your vision and your goals. Petraeus found many opportunities to visit troops on the battlefield, and he was relentless about communication at all levels. The intention was always the same: to help people to understand what they were doing, and why it mattered. "I only made about 12 decisions during the war," I heard Petraeus say. It struck me at that moment because the number was so low. He had communicated the objectives clearly. Through that communication, he transferred decision-making to his Lieutenants and other commanders in the field. Leadership was distributed, not guarded. Want to know if you are a good leader? Start giving leadership away. Be clear in what you need and give people the opportunity to use their own mental horsepower to make decisions. Course-correct along the way. Petraeus was clear in the transfer of ownership and decision-making, because he had to be. Petraeus said, "implementing big ideas typically requires empowering people and organizations to execute the ideas at their levels without the need for constant approval – indeed, empowering subordinate leaders to exercise considerable initiative." This doctrine is called "mission command" - a disciplined initiative to empower leaders who are agile, adaptive and responsible.

2. **Consider Untapped Resources:** William Ury, one of the co-authors of the business classic, *Getting to Yes,*

says in his latest book, *Possible,* that we have to look beyond the traditional "win-win" solution. Ury says that there is always a third side, in any conflict. That means you can create a "win-win-win", and in today's world, that's what we all need. The third side, according to Ury, is represented by community. A conflict will not stand if the community at large will not stand for it. "The third side is a sleeping giant," Ury writes. "The third side is the power to swarm - to apply a critical mass of ideas and influence... [The third side] is a latent 'superpower' that exists within each and all of us. Our challenge today is to find ways to wake it up." For the TABC, we considered the untapped resources of the beverage distributors across the State. We enrolled a larger community in an initiative that served the greater good. As a leader, what is it that you can say or share that mobilizes a larger community? What is that "third side" that remains dormant, until you activate it? How can you make sure that you are communicating with your team, to make them aware of the fact that they are a part of something special, important and meaningful? Because when you win, the marketplace wins. Your constituents win. Your team wins. Look for "win-win-win" and you're looking in the direction of untapped resources. It's easy to be cynical and say, "Well, making software doesn't change the world" or "Selling tractors and farm machinery doesn't make a difference." Unless you are a farmer. Or someone who uses that aforementioned software. Because what you are doing *definitely* makes a difference for the customers you serve. The people on your team. Or the constituents who voted for you. Not every business is trying to cure cancer - but inside every enterprise is the opportunity to serve. Identify that service, share it within a community, and you are tapping into powerful resources.

3. **Create a Learning Organization:** Petraeus was in charge of the Center for Army Lessons Learned - a place where "lessons" were not just observed, they were institutionalized. Because a forgotten lesson, on the battlefield, can have tragic consequences. In business, forgotten lessons are lost opportunities - and can be very expensive. Mistakes can be costly. Repeated mistakes are unaffordable. As it has been said, those who do not study history are doomed to repeat it. As a leader, consider the lessons that matter most - and create a learning culture that reinforces valuable history. Combine the instruction of the past with an opportunity for building the future. In other words, make space for new ideas, and train people so that they understand what's needed (and they are empowered to deliver it). Deliver training programs and learning, so that new ideas become new behaviors. Exposure to new ideas is vital to the growth of any organization - and the growth of your people. A learning organization captures best practices and institutionalizes them. At TABC, we implemented a leadership training program so that staff members knew what leadership really looked like. Candidly, some of the team members didn't really understand what the organization needed. But how can people deliver something, if they don't learn what it is, how it works, and how to turn knowledge into new behaviors? Don't assume that having an advanced degree or decades of experience means

that learning is unnecessary. They say you can't teach an old dog new tricks. But that really depends on the dog, the trainer, and the trick. Beyond the clever clichés, advanced insights can come to anyone, at any time. If that were not true, people would never change, and grow. Even the most educated person has something to learn, if they remain open to that discovery. As a leader, your role is to identify where learning needs to occur - and work to make sure that a spirit of openness and learning permeates the organization. Create a conduit of culture, based on growth through new learning. And remember that growth always comes from insight, not a lecture. We take in information, but insight is what creates real change. For example, everyone who smokes cigarettes knows the implications of nicotine, and the risks of disease, from tobacco. That information - that knowledge - is readily available. But what makes someone stop smoking? Sometimes more information makes people dig in even harder to an existing choice. Sometimes information - even wise counsel from scientists and experts - can be dismissed. Ultimately, changing course comes from an insight. That insight can be a simple thought. A thought that says, "It doesn't have to be like this." Can you create a space for that kind of insight? The learning organization says, "What else could this be?" Whether you are changing a personal habit, or changing a multinational company, remember: insight is the key. The learning culture activates insight, explores possibility, and offers team members an opportunity to share and contribute what they are seeing. Because none of us is as smart as all of us. So, make sure your education doesn't just stop at information - make room for insights, and make learning a top priority.

4. **Course Correction is Available:** Perfectionism is the enemy of action. As leaders, we almost never have complete information. Waiting for perfect information is a fool's errand, especially when decisions need to be made. Every leader wants to make the right decision. But what makes a decision "right"? The answer is: you do. You have the ability to make a decision, and to make that decision right - by your actions, your insights, and by course correcting as needed. Decisions never exist in isolation - you have to follow your shot, teach people what they need to learn, hold people accountable. Stop looking for the "right" way to do something and expecting that someone else's template will fit into your life, your business or your career. Ask yourself: Is there more than one way to win? Do second chances exist? Yes, they do. I got a second chance, when that shell hit the shower trailer outside of Baghdad. It wasn't my time. And that fact made me appreciate the time that I have. Dwight Eisenhower famously said, "Every battle is going to surprise you. No plan ever survives its first contact with the enemy." That's why you have to keep fighting, keep adjusting, and keep on learning. Hold people accountable for the standard of excellence you have set, and you have taught. But stay flexible! Welcome new ideas, go on patrol and see what's really happening (not just what you think is happening). Remember that adaptability is a critical skill for all of us – and a capacity that we all possess. Remain rigid and you miss an

opportunity - for yourself and your team. The leader that wins is the leader that adapts. Balance your commitment with an understanding that your vision must change, as the terrain, players and obstacles are changing. Remind yourself and remind your team: we have to work hard to make a decision right, and continually make decisions that lead towards excellence.

TAKE ACTION:

From the stories shared in this chapter, several key leadership strategies and initiatives emerge, providing valuable lessons for managers, executives, and corporate founders:

INNOVATION AND ADAPTABILITY:

- Initiative: Recognizing the need for a new approach, the Texas Alcoholic Beverage Commission (TABC) took the initiative to address the human trafficking issue by developing the first-of-its-kind human trafficking undercover school.

- Lesson: Leaders should encourage innovative thinking and be willing to adapt their strategies to address emerging challenges effectively.

COLLABORATION AND PARTNERSHIPS:

- Partnership with Beer Distributors: TABC collaborated with beer distributors, turning them into an unconventional but highly effective resource for identifying human trafficking activities in bars and other establishments.
- Lesson: Leaders should explore partnerships with unexpected allies, tapping into untapped resources to amplify their impact.

EMPLOYEE TRAINING AND EDUCATION:

- Undercover School: TABC initiated a human trafficking undercover school, where survivors of human trafficking played a crucial role in training agents.
- Lesson: Leaders should invest in continuous training for their teams, leveraging the expertise of those directly impacted by the issues at hand for a more informed and empathetic approach.

COMMUNICATION AND CULTURE:

- Communication with Beer Truck Drivers: Clear communication with beer truck drivers enabled them to serve as a mobile task force, reporting suspicious activities.

- Lesson: Leaders must prioritize clear communication to create a shared understanding of organizational goals and foster a culture of shared responsibility.

RISK-TAKING AND COURAGE:

- Press Conference Announcement: TABC took on the challenge of addressing human trafficking issues and criminal activities, demonstrating the courage to tackle a complex problem head-on.
- Lesson: Leaders should be willing to take risks and confront challenges directly, even when it involves stepping outside the traditional scope of their responsibilities.

LEARNING ORGANIZATION:

- Leadership Training Program: TABC implemented a leadership training program, emphasizing the importance of continuous learning and adapting to new challenges.
- Lesson: Leaders should cultivate a learning culture within their organizations, promoting an openness to new ideas and a willingness to adapt based on insights gained from experience.

FLEXIBILITY AND COURSE CORRECTION:

- Response to Increased Reports: TABC experienced a 700% increase in human trafficking reports and adjusted its priorities accordingly.
- Lesson: Leaders should be flexible, willing to course-

correct, and recognize that adaptability is essential in a dynamic environment.

MISSION COMMAND AND EMPOWERMENT:

- General Petraeus's Leadership Approach: TABC drew inspiration from General Petraeus's mission command approach, empowering subordinates to take initiative. How are you transferring leadership, and ownership, into your organization?
- Lesson: Leaders should empower their teams, distributing decision-making authority and fostering a sense of ownership among team members.

COMMUNITY ENGAGEMENT AND THE "THIRD SIDE":

- Wholesale Beer Distributors of America Encouragement: TABC's success prompted other states to adopt similar programs, showcasing the power of community engagement. Who is the "third side" that could help you, in your current initiatives?
- Lesson: Leaders should consider the broader community impact of their initiatives, aiming for "win-win-win" solutions that benefit not only the organization but also the community at large.

CONTINUOUS IMPROVEMENT AND EXCELLENCE:

TABC's ability to adjust its strategies based on insights and changing circumstances contributed to its success in combating human trafficking. Do you need a course correction, right now? Does your organization?

Leaders should prioritize continuous improvement, viewing mistakes as opportunities for learning and growth, and striving for excellence in their endeavors.

By incorporating these leadership strategies and lessons, you can enhance your ability to address complex challenges, foster innovation, and create a positive impact on both your organization, and the broader community.

7

FROM VISION TO VICTORY:

CREATING A LASTING LEGACY

"Legacy is not leaving something for people. It's leaving something in people." - Peter Strople, American Philanthropist and Conscious Capitalist

"The greatest legacy one can pass on to one's children and grandchildren is not money or other material things accumulated in one's life, but rather a legacy of character and faith." - Billy Graham, American Evangelist

Will you leave this world better than you found it?

Creating excellence isn't just a personal pursuit. Excellence, like leadership, responsibility and integrity, is meant to be shared. Shared in the spirit of creating something new. Something that builds on the past but expands into the future. Something that's bigger than you are.

Every day, as I write in this book, I remember that we are all writing our own stories. Our own legacies. My legacy is something that will be remembered by my two sons, long after I'm gone. And so, creating excellence is something I have sought my whole life. How about you?

When I became a founding member of Brazos Valley Cares, I did it because I wanted to help veterans. Brazos Valley Cares is a non-profit organization, dedicated to helping veterans with housing and other emergency needs. I got involved because it needed to be done.

Reflecting back on my life, that's why I served my country. My state. And also, my community. Because I saw a need. For Brazos Valley Cares, the organization created an emergency hotline for veterans needing short-term financial assistance. We created funding for crucial life events, so that service men and women could access a helping hand when money got tight. We provide connections for veterans, and support for our community. I'm proud to say that the organization is run entirely by volunteers - people who share a commitment to those who have served. And 100% of all money raised goes towards our mission. With a population just under 250,000 people, Brazos County is better off because of the veterans who live and contribute here. And I'd like to think that the veterans are better off, because of Brazos Valley Cares.

A lot of organizations, especially non-profit organizations, don't survive a transition in leadership. Legacy is about creating something that survives change, including personnel changes. Inside any organization, your most valuable asset is going to be your human capital.

It's interesting how our mission wasn't about creating a legacy, really. But that's what evolved, in retrospect - because we were creating excellence. And others picked up the commitment, joining forces to create something that is ever evolving and always improving.

People took the original idea of serving veterans in times of need - the core value of the organization - and expanded it, over the years. If you are interested in leaving a legacy, you must be deliberate about creating a culture of excellence. That doesn't mean you build something just so you can put your name on it. Far from it. When you focus on the mission, and find others who share your values, you're working for the greater good. That's the place where ideas can thrive, and innovation builds on the past to advance the mission. It's really not about my history, when I think of legacy. Recognition is sometimes the after-effect, but never the intention.

I'm a blip on the history of any organization I serve. But the organization, Brazos Valley Cares, continues.

That's because there are people in my community who care about helping veterans and their families to thrive. Over the years, new volunteers have brought new ideas - creating outdoor events, jewelry shows, and inventive ideas to bring families together. As a veteran living in Brazos County, I want this place to be a welcoming home for military men and women. So far, the organization has offered over $600,000 in veteran assistance, $400,000 in grants, and over 1000 hotline call responses. In 2023, Brazos Valley Cares introduced a new Mental Health Initiative with plans to partner with several local licensed therapists specializing in service-related trauma, anxiety and depression as well as organizations offering non-traditional therapy services such as equine therapy, outdoor family retreats, and Hyperbaric Oxygen Treatment for invisible wounds like PTSD and Traumatic Brain Injury.

The Brazos Valley is also home to the largest university in the United States, Texas A&M. The largest in terms of student population, as well as land mass, the campus sprawls over 5,200 acres. The school is steeped in traditions - maybe more so than any other university in our nation. Home to over 75,000 Aggie students, Aggieland is a part of me, just as I am a part of the community that lives here.

.   .   .

"There's a Spirit can ne'er be told..."
The Spirit of Aggieland

THE *WALL STREET JOURNAL* ranked Texas A&M as the number one university in the Lone Star State, and the sixth in the nation among all public universities for 2024. What's behind this legacy? (https://tinyurl.com/creatingexcellence7-1)

"From the outside looking in, you can't understand it. And from the inside looking out, you can't explain it."
- famous quote about Texas A&M, Anonymous

ONE OF THE rich traditions of Texas A&M is the idea of the 12th man.

The tradition of the Twelfth Man was born over 100 years ago. On the second of January 1922, an underdog Aggie team was playing Centre College, then the nation's top ranked team. As the hard-fought game wore on, and the Aggies dug deeply into their limited reserves, Coach Dana X. Bible remembered a squad man who was not in uniform. He had been up in the press box helping reporters identify players. His name was E. King Gill and was a former football player who was only playing basketball. Gill was called from the stands, suited up, and stood ready throughout the rest of the game, which A&M finally won. When the game ended, E. King Gill was the only man left standing on the sidelines for the Aggies. Gill later said, "I wish I could say that I went in and ran for the winning touchdown, but I did not. I simply stood by in case my team needed me."

. . .

W̲HAT DOES YOUR TEAM NEED, right now? What do you stand for?

In the sprawling landscape of higher education, where institutions strive for excellence, Chancellor John Sharp represents the best of the Texas A&M System. His visionary leadership has propelled Texas A&M to the forefront of academia.

The Board of Regents appointed John Sharp as Chancellor in 2011. Today, he leads one of the largest educational systems in the country with an annual budget of $7.8 billion and an enrollment of more than 153,000 students at 11 System universities. Additionally, under the System umbrella, there are eight state agencies. Sharp is no stranger to government and politics in Texas, having served in both houses of the Legislature, as well as being elected State Comptroller for two terms.

I had the privilege of speaking with the Chancellor to talk about his legacy.

"Creating excellence means whatever moves an institution forward towards its goals," Sharp says, matter-of-factly. His conversational style is humble, self-effacing...and focused. "If your goals are to create more research, better opportunities, whatever moves your agency or business forward, design your organization to do what you need it to do."

S̲HARP SITS at a dark wooden table, surrounded by four chairs. On either side of him are two mounted deer heads, both multi-point bucks, watching over our conversation. An antique portrait of Madonna with Child is framed on the wall. Its yellow, gold and blue colors stand out against the dark wood that surrounds the Chancellor. On the floor beneath the painting, a carved statue of an eagle in flight spreads its tan wooden wing-span - nearly five feet across. On the other side of the expansive office, the same color of dark wood defines the space. Curios fill the built-in shelves with memories of his service, accomplishments and accolades.

Sharp attended Texas A&M during a time of transition for the university, graduating in 1972. He served in the Corps of Cadets, a longstanding tradition at the school, and served as student body president.

With a career like his, I asked him, what has been your greatest accomplishment?

"My grandchildren," he says, with a laugh. He follows that answer with a reflection on his biggest leadership influence: "My wife - that's always a safe answer."

On a more serious note, he reflects on a professional influence: one of the giants in Texas politics. Bill Moore, known as the Bull of the Brazos, was Sharp's first boss. Moore, a state legislator across three decades, was often called "the most powerful man in state government", because he was able to get the Senate to follow his lead. You couldn't get a bill passed in the State without Bill Moore's support, at one point in time. Like Sharp, Moore was influential in politics - and a tremendous supporter of Texas A&M.

Bob Cherry, a former assistant chancellor at Texas A&M, called Moore "the father of the modern Texas A&M University." Indeed, Moore introduced historic legislation that allowed women to attend the school for the first time. And when it came to integrating the historically white college, Moore told the Texas Governor, John Connally, that he would not vote to confirm any appointee to the Texas A&M Board of Regents who did not favor coeducational status. During a time of racial tension across the US, Texas A&M also began accepting students of color in the early 1960s.

When Sharp came to A&M, he put on his accounting hat - and transformed the budget of multi-million-dollar entities within the universities. "That was the first thing I saw when I started going over the budget," Sharp told *Texas Monthly*. "Administrators hire administrators. If you're going to be an administrator, you want to supervise a lot of people. It's like rules and regulations—where do those come from? They come from bureaucrats who want to justify their jobs.

"This has been the most liberating experience of my life," Sharp told *Texas Monthly*, referring to his appointment as Chancellor. "After I left politics, I made enough money so that I don't have to have this job. So I can truly do what Sam Houston said, which is do right and hell with the consequences."

"I THINK that once you get into a mode where you don't have to worry about the consequences," Sharp elaborated, "you can see that 'hey, this is something we ought to do'. No matter what dogs are barking and raising hell about it, as long as you are comfortable, it's right." I admire his confidence. "Just do it, and don't look back."

I wondered if that means that he just acts with impunity, or without regard for how other people are going to react or respond? After all, I know that Sharp is one of the most connected and well-networked people in the entire State. He's neither an autocrat nor a fool. So, his answer - "to hell with the consequences" - surprised me. Surely, he knows the significance of building a vast network of friends and allies, emphasizing the role of collaboration in achieving institutional goals? Maybe it's the strength of his network that strengthens his decision-making?

"One of the things that my dad taught me a long time ago -

when I was a shy little grade-schooler - is that you can never have too many friends," Sharp confides. "I'm very much aware of the fact that you can't do very much by yourself. You have to have people that can help you to enable your vision, people that you can rely on to provide you with advice. You use all the tools you have, to make sure you're able to get things done through federal and state agencies. What I meant by Sam Houston's quote is that once you reach a point where somebody's standing in the way, and you're absolutely sure you're right, move forward. Do it." Shelves of awards and pictures with State leaders watch over his words, a testimony to his commitment to friends - and to decisive action.

THE LEGACY UNVEILED

From the creation of a law school to the elevation of faculty through National Academy memberships, Chancellor Sharp's leadership exemplifies a commitment to excellence. Early in his tenure, he oversaw the refurbishment of Kyle Field, a half-billion-dollar project that updated the school's football stadium - replacing parts of the stadium that dated all the way back to 1927.

"What we are about is solving problems," Sharp continues, zooming out to look at the big picture - a particular skill of his. "We're building a facility for NASA to replicate the surface of the moon and Mars, so that NASA and private entities can do surface research that's not enabled anywhere else in the country."

Sharp's vision for the University expands beyond the boundaries of our planet. "There was a lack of engineers," he told me, describing more about what needed to be done to enable a wider ability to build programs for the future. "So we've become the largest engineering university in the country," Sharp says.

Government entities love to form committees, he reminds me. I nod in agreement and can't help but chuckle to myself. We both reflect on how analysis paralysis can be the enemy of progress. Inside an academic institution, where delay is *de rigeur*, Sharp advocates for a kind of guided impatience in the pursuit of excellence. So how does he create progress inside a system that isn't necessarily designed to quickly accept it?

"We say, 'it's a good idea. Do it'," he says, simply. "And if somebody is lagging behind, we take it away and give it to someone else who will make it work. We are impatient," he admits, "and that actually helps."

THE VISION FOR THE FUTURE

Ten miles north of the Chancellor's office, the 2,000-acre RELLIS Campus is a big part of Sharp's legacy. Sharing his vision with the Army Futures Command back in 2018, Sharp led the university to build a one-of-a-kind hypersonic missile testing facility. Sharp envisioned this testing facility in 2018. US military officials have long believed that our country is behind China and Russia, in terms of high-speed missile technology. Sharp is working hard to change that. As of this writing, 20 one-kilometer-long tubes are being embedded deep in the ground - providing a 12-mile test facility for projectiles that can travel up to 10 times the speed of sound. Tim Green, Director of the Bush Combat Development Complex at RELLIS, says that the supersonic initiative is about preserving the freedom of US citizens. "The weapons that we have simply don't give us enough options," he says. "This is about saving American lives. The lives of American soldiers. It's about protecting our national interest here in the United States."

At the launch of the RELLIS Campus, Sharp told media and reporters, "The RELLIS Campus presented us with an opportunity to lead the way in redefining research and education. The world-class facilities here will ensure the next generation of Texas will benefit from everything the Texas A&M System can offer."

THE AGGIE SPIRIT: CONNECTIONS AND SERVICE

RELLIS is an acronym for the six core values at Texas A&M: Respect, Excellence, Leadership, Loyalty, Integrity, and Selfless Service. These core values are known to every Aggie, and exemplify the experience purpose, for every Texas A&M student and alum. What do these values represent for you, and your organization?

RESPECT - Born of friendliness, caring, support, confidence - and a can-do attitude

EXCELLENCE: SET THE BAR - "Excellence stems from a great sense of pride in who we are and what we believe in." -Former Texas A&M president, Dr. Robert Gates

LOYALTY: ACCEPTANCE FOREVER - The motto of the Texas A&M Corps of Cadets: *Through unity, strength.*

LEADERSHIP - Whether you go on to lead in the boardroom or the backyard, you experience the values, confidence and experience to lead change in your world.

INTEGRITY: BECAUSE CHARACTER IS DESTINY - The Aggie Code of Honor: "Aggies do not lie, cheat or steal nor tolerate those who do."

SELFLESS SERVICE -"A&M encourages volunteerism, encourages being

one of a thousand points of light, helping others...and it comes natu-
rally to Aggies." - Former US President, George H. W. Bush

I ASKED THE CHANCELLOR, other than "leadership" (which might be considered his job description) what's your favorite core value?

"Loyalty," he said, without hesitation.

Indeed, it is his loyalty to his alma mater, and his commitment to selfless service, that drives his leadership. From core values comes an action plan, and a vision for the future. John Sharp is creating excellence. And with another four years on his contract, his legacy is still taking shape.

During the writing of this book, Sharp announced that he will be retiring from A&M in 2025. But I suspect his presence will be felt for many years to come.

For John Sharp, legacy requires commitment. That's why he celebrates loyalty, in his pursuit of excellence. Loyalty is where he finds dedication - as well as the will to move quickly. Because, like the projects he's working on for the University right now, that's what needs to be done.

TAKE ACTION:

From the stories shared in this chapter, reflect on your legacy. What will you leave behind? How are you leaving things better than you found them? Consider these areas, where you can begin creating excellence.

1. **Find the Value inside Your Values:** Consider the core values that drive your personal and professional life. At Texas A&M, the core values are written on buildings, and woven into the fabric of the university experience. What are your core values? How do these values align with the principles of excellence and legacy-building?

2. **Your Network is Your Net Worth:** Reflect on your connections and network. Consider the balance between support, decisions, and action. How do your current relationships contribute to your journey toward achieving your goals?

3. **Determination and Decision-Making:** What's that one decision that you've been putting off, for whatever reason, because you're worried about

popular opinion, or public resistance? Doing what's right doesn't mean it's easy. What's the simplest step you could take, today, to create a new legacy? What challenges do you foresee on your path to excellence, and how can you approach them with the same determination as Chancellor John Sharp?

4. **Seeing Selfless Service:** In what ways can you embody the spirit of service in your endeavors, inspired by the Aggie culture highlighted in the chapter?

5. **Embodying Loyalty:** The traditions at A&M run deep. Do you have traditions for yourself, your company, or your family? Forward-thinking leaders build on tradition by introducing innovation. What does loyalty mean to you? What could you do to deepen your relationships and your commitments, so that loyalty isn't just a concept - but an action plan, for your future?

6. **Putting plans into action** - that's a mark of a leader. Creating excellence means not only having a plan but turning that plan into a reality.

You now know how to build your plan, negotiate with those who may not see things the same way you do, and even how to enter into enemy territory and prepare for the unexpected. From Chancellor Sharp's story, you understand the importance of vision and purpose - as well as the importance of relationships.

Remember: you are capable of dealing with the unexpected, and so are your teammates. Our final chapter looks at what's ahead, as the future remains unknown - and unexpected. As the saying goes, "Every moment is a fresh beginning," according to the poet, T. S. Eliot. Which means that, while this chapter is coming to an end, your journey is just getting started.

Nettles unseats Aldrich in County Commissioner Precinct 1 Republican primary runoff

I was a tight race.

I've served my country, and my state. The next level of service, for me, is service to my local community. Over the years, I've been entrusted with some of the most precious resources in this country: namely, serving and protecting the men, women and children who live here. My service is not done, however.

And that's why I wanted to run for office, in my local community.

Three candidates entered the race for the County Commissioner's position. After the votes were counted, three became two. But at that point, the election was too close to call. The incumbent and I went into a runoff election. What happened next surprised everyone.

The incumbent put up a formidable campaign, and I respect his efforts. But the runoff was a runaway success. Never before in the history of Brazos County had there been a double-digit margin of victory in a runoff election. And, thanks to the support of the voters, that's what I received. It was the widest margin in any runoff election, for any position, in the county. Ever.

Now the work really begins. The opportunity to serve my community is what I anticipate as the next chapter in my life.

Writing this book, however, has been an amazing experience. The mission, for me, is what matters.

And that mission continues. Not just for me. But for you as well. Where will you be creating excellence, in your life and in your career?

My hope is that this book has helped you to see that excellence isn't something "out there". Excellence isn't something that's reserved for military leaders, state officials or business executives. Excellence is within you. On your life journey, remember that we all have the capacity to create excellence. Give your best to your life. To your relationships. To your career.

Never forget that excellence is within your reach - and the reach of those around you. Holding people to a higher standard, when it is done with compassion and dedication, is the ultimate expression of leadership. Are you willing to let that expression come through, for you?

Self-leadership is the first step.

Remember to bring your excellence to bear on whatever

circumstance you are facing - including the way that you treat yourself. It's easy to fall into a trap of negative self-talk - the kind of internal dialogue that is filled with what you have forgotten.

"The kingdom of heaven is within you," the Good Book says (Luke 17:20-21). And I believe it. Consider a message for both believers and non-believers alike: the same spark that turns acorns into oak trees and makes waves hit the shore is inside of you. That's not motivational mumbo-jumbo. That's the way the universe works. And that spark of innovation - of new ideas - is the one resource that never runs out.

Don't forget what you are made of, don't forget who you are. Excellence is inside of you.

In the workplace, on the home front, in your negotiations and your collaborations, create excellence. When you serve, do so with your full heart. Commit to see beyond the noise, the gossip and the conflict - because the world needs your excellence. Be the bearer of truth and bring integrity to every conversation - even when it's not easy.

I'm reminded of a children's song, from many years ago. A song that I have heard sung in church hallways, and vacation bible schools, ringing out in young voices. The message is simple, the reminder profound.

~

> This little light of mine
> I'm gonna let it shine

~

Let your light shine, my friend. Let that spark that is inside of you be of service to the people you care about. If you are fortunate enough to serve your country, your state or your community, do so with a commitment that lets your light shine. In business, honor your commitments. Honor your family, with your work and your service and your spirit and your attention. Bring service and clarity to your team, your customers, and your shareholders. This is the job that you are uniquely qualified to fulfill:

KEEP CREATING EXCELLENCE, wherever you go.

~

Bentley Nettles, Brigadier General (BVT)

ACKNOWLEDGMENTS

Thank You

This book would not have been possible without the support of my community, in and around Brazos County. To my friends at the Texas Alcoholic Beverage Commission, I thank you.

I am deeply grateful to my wife, Tracy, and to my boys for their love and encouragement.

A special shoutout to Chris Westfall, for helping me to bring this story to life. Appreciate your support.

To the men and women who served with me, those who are still with us and those who have gone on to the other side, I thank you for all that you have done.

Finally, to my state, my county, and my country - with sincere appreciation for all that you have given me.

www.ingramcontent.com/pod-product-compliance
Lightning Source LLC
Chambersburg PA
CBHW061315120726
48001CB00002B/510